SCHOLASTIC
YEAR IN SPORTS
2026
I0820640

ISBN 979-8-225-00503-0

10 9 8 7 6 5 4 3 2 25 26 27 28 29

Printed in the U.S.A. 40
First edition, December 2025

Produced by Shoreline Publishing Group LLC

Due to the publication date, records, results, and statistics are current as of mid-July 2025.

Contents

Sports Never Sleeps!

On what days of the year are there no pro sports? The answer used to be the days before and after the MLB All-Star Game. Back then, baseball was the only sport left in the summer after the NHL and NBA ended. The NFL season hadn't begun yet, either. So for those two days, sports were on a timeout! But today, the answer to that that question is . . . *none*! There are pro sports events in the United States every single day of the year from January 1 to December 31! And we've got all 365 of those days in this book!

Clark fired up hoops fans in 2024!

What changed? Well, one big difference is women's sports. Basketball's WNBA and soccer's NWSL play throughout the summer. They often have games on those once-empty days. In fact, the growth in popularity of women's pro sports has been one of the biggest stories of recent years. College women athletes have been getting more attention, too, with the NCAA basketball tournament getting big ratings and college softball drawing fans to national TV.

So sports is nonstop, all year long, and we've got it all in these pages.

The NFL is still the biggest game in town, with more fans and higher ratings than anything. The Super Bowl was the most-watched TV program of 2025, period. Not just among sports shows but ALL shows.

And the game was worth watching, as you can find out in our NFL chapter.

The "boys of summer" (that's a nickname for baseball players) put on another great show in 2024, featuring one of the best hitting seasons of all time . . . and **Shohei Ohtani**, too! Find out how Shohei won his first World Series ring in the pages ahead.

Jalen Hurts got the hardware in 2025!

One of the biggest names in this past sports year was **Caitlin Clark**, who joined the Indiana Fever of the WNBA after her amazing college career. She was under the spotlight, but she came through big-time in 2024 with one of the best rookie seasons ever. But she didn't bring home the top trophy; that went to the New York Liberty and **Breanna Stewart**.

The NBA featured a new champ for the seventh season in a row. The Oklahoma City Thunder, led by the awesome **Shai Gilgeous-Alexander**, had one of the best seasons in league history. They capped it off with the 2025 championship.

The Orlando Pride were the NWSL champs, while the LA Galaxy won Major League Soccer. Speaking of the world's most popular sport, there were some amazing results from Europe, from the top men's and women's leagues to the Champions League. How did your favorite "football" teams do?

And there was so much more . . . the calendar was overflowing! We've got all the news from motor sports, tennis, golf, skiing, figure skating, and canal-jumping. Wait, what? Keep reading to find out!

No matter how you spend your day, here's hoping you make sports part of it, either watching, playing, or reading! Make it a sporty year!

The YEAR IN SPORTS AWARDS!

They're back! The Sportys return to honor things in sports that probably didn't get any other trophies. Winners of all sorts get plaques and statues and medals. MVPs are honored, along with other players of the year. But the Sportys are here to make sure that some other fun things about sports are remembered. Our time period is from August 2024 to July 2025. Fun or funny, memorable or just odd . . . here are the 2025 Sportys!

MVB: MOST VALUABLE BEEKEEPER

Before a game in Arizona, the Dodgers and Diamondbacks needed help. Call the beekeeper! A huge swarm of bees was hanging out behind home plate. Bee expert **Matt Hilton** showed up and removed the swarm as the fans cheered. Hilton got to throw out the first pitch . . . and later even had a baseball card made of him!

Hilton used smoke to calm the bees before removing them.

Wilson (before the red card)

WEIRDEST RED CARD EVER!

Soccer players who earn a second yellow card caution also get a red card. They are kicked out of the game and can't be replaced. Portland Thorns star **Sophia Smith Wilson** might have earned the oddest red card ever. She was on the bench late in a game against the NC Courage. When the ball went out of bounds, Smith sort of, well . . . she tried to hide the ball to delay a throw-in for the Courage! The ref spotted it and gave her a second yellow card. Yes, you can get one even on the bench! That made it a red for the day, and she had to miss the team's next game.

BEST USE OF A HAT (NOT ON HEAD)

Appearing in 62 games in 2024, relief pitcher **Cionel Pérez** spent a lot of time in the Baltimore Orioles bullpen, waiting to be called to the mound. He developed a new hobby—catching home runs in his cap! Pérez managed to snag six homers during the season, which, as far as we know, is a record!

Pérez also had 2 saves and 2 wins.

THE LONG WAIT AWARD

San Marino is one of the tiniest countries in the world. It's surrounded by Italy and is home to only 34,000 citizens. But it still has a national soccer team . . . just not a very good one. But those folks got some major joy in September 2024. Their team beat Liechtenstein (another tiny country) 1-0. It was San Marino's first international win in 20 years! The W broke a streak of 140 games that it had not won (there were some ties). They topped it all by moving up a spot in the Nations League in 2025. Never give up, right?

San Marino finally won!

SO CLOSE AND YET SO FAR AWARD

Um, Malachi? You forgot something!

It's a basic part of football. You have to carry the ball into the end zone to earn a touchdown. **Braden Marshall** of Central Florida missed that lesson and made a mistake we're sure he'll never repeat! Just before crossing the goal line after a 70-yard interception return, he started to celebrate and let go of the ball. Oops. His team did keep the ball and scored on the next play. New York Jets receiver **Malachi Corley** was not so lucky. His dropped "almost TD" went for a touchback to the opposing team.

THE STICK-WITH-IT AWARD

The celebration of a surprise champion!

Oklahoma State wrestler **Wyatt Hendrickson** knew his opponent, **Gable Steveson** of Minnesota, very well. Steveson had won the college national title twice and even had an Olympic gold medal! *And* he had beaten Hendrickson 18-2 in a previous meet. But Hendrickson didn't care. He just wanted to win. In what one writer called "the most shocking result in NCAA wrestling history," Hendrickson beat Steveson 5-4 to win the 2025 NCAA heavyweight title.

THE BUSY SCOREKEEPER AWARD

There was good news and bad news for the Louisville women's volleyball team. The bad news was that they lost the NCAA championship match to Penn State. The good news was that they won a game for the ages. Most indoor volleyball games end at 25 points. But you have to win by two points, so sometimes games go a few points further. The third game of this match didn't want to end! The teams needed a total of 66 points, an NCAA championship record. The Cardinals won the game 34-32 but lost the match to the Nittany Lions.

Louisville (in red) survived a long Game 3.

THE CHAMPIONSHIP SELFIE AWARD

Hey, trophy! Say cheese, please!

This book is filled with awesome photos taken by the best sports photographers in the world. This picture, however, shows an athlete taking care of his own photo needs. **Joey Logano** posed for a selfie after winning the 2024 NASCAR Cup championship.
He didn't share it with us, so here's a pic of him . . . taking a pic!

PUT THIS COACH IN A TIMEOUT AWARD

The action late in a tight NBA game can be pretty wild. So we might give Miami Heat head coach **Erik Spoelstra** a little slack. But he made a pretty big error late in his team's game with the Detroit Pistons. With the game tied and 1.1 seconds left, he called timeout. He wanted to set up a play for his team. One problem: The Heat was out of timeouts. The Pistons made the technical foul free throws and won the game 123-121. Oops.

Sorry, Coach . . . no more TOs for you!

Curry says goodbye to dunks!

THE END OF DUNKS AWARD

Stephen Curry of the Golden State Warriors is one of the greatest scorers ever in basketball. He has poured in thousands of points in his 16-year career. However, he made nearly all of them while only very rarely dunking. In a March 2025 game against Philadelphia, he rose up to dunk home this basket, his first slam since 2019. After the game, he said, "That will probably be my last dunk." We're glad we got to see it!

THE TRY, TRY, TRY AGAIN AWARD

San Francisco 49ers kicker **Jake Moody** missed *three* field goals in his team's game against the Tampa Bay Buccaneers. But a tough day ended on a good note. He got one more chance on the game's final play. He nailed a 44-yard kick to win the game 23-20. Just stick with it, sports fans!

Moody changed Niners fans' mood with this kick!

THE MINI-AWARD FOR A MINI-HOOPSTER

A JuJu Funko is ready to play!

When the USC Trojans took the court to play Kansas State in the NCAA tournament, they had a unique "teammate." Standing on the court with the players was a 5-inch tall Funko Pop! toy in the shape of USC's **JuJu Watkins**. The superstar had been hurt in the previous game. The toy was there to honor her and inspire her teammates. It must have worked—the Trojans beat the Wildcats 67-61!

THE "THAT'S ONE EXPENSIVE JERSEY" AWARD

This No. 22 cost Juan Soto a new car!

Athletes can be pretty superstitious about their uniform numbers. So when the great **Juan Soto** joined the New York Mets, he wanted to wear No. 22 like he always had. But the Mets' **Brett Baty** already wore that number. Being a good teammate (and knowing how much Soto would help his team), Baty gave Soto the number. A few weeks later, to say thanks, Soto gave Baty a brand-new car! Don't worry, he can afford it. Soto signed with the Mets for $765 million!

THE MOST AMAZING ACTUAL SPORT AWARD

There are so many awesome sports in the world! Here's one that you will probably not think is real . . . but it is. It's hobby horsing. A hobby horse is a toy horse on a stick. In the sport, people gallop around with the toy and do horse-event-like things. They do jumps and dressage (which is like horse ballet) and even barrel racing. Why? Why not?

A hobby horse athlete leaps . . . like a horse!

THE EVERYONE'S A WINNER AWARD

Yeshiva's Jacob Canner celebrates the end of a long streak!

Baseball fans in New York City got to see something pretty special in April 2025. Two college teams that had long losing streaks both saw them end . . . on the same day . . . against each other! How can that happen? Thanks to a doubleheader, that's how. Lehman College won the first game, ending its 42-game losing streak. Then Yeshiva University won the second game, ending a 100-game string without a W. Smiles all around!

2024 PARALYMPICS

MAGNIFIQUE!
The 2024 Paralympics opened with a great Opening Ceremony, right in the heart of beautiful Paris. Jets flew overhead, singers and dancers performed, and the athletes marched in. Here's the US team, led by flag bearers Nicky Nieves (sitting volleyball) and Steve Serio (wheelchair basketball).

2024 Paralympics

In late August 2024, the Paralympics filled the streets and stadiums of Paris with incredible athletes. More than 4,400 Paralympians from 170 teams took part in the Games, held every four years after the Summer Olympics. Millions of fans cheered them on. At one track event, the crowd got so loud that the athletes had to ask them to settle down so they could concentrate! (In the Paralympics, athletes compete against others who have the same level of physical or visual ability. That means there are often several races of the same length, with different levels of athletes in each.)

At sites around Paris, the athletes showed off their skills. Some Americans added to their career Paralympic success. **Jessica Long**'s two medals in Paris moved her career total to 31, the most ever by an active Paralympic swimmer. Wheelchair racer **Tatyana McFadden** moved to 21 career medals, the top American ever, just ahead of fellow track star **Oksana Masters**, who left Paris with 19 career medals. (She had earlier earned medals in skiing and rowing, too!) **Hunter Woodhall** ran to a 400-meter gold, giving his family two wins in '24. His wife, **Tara Davis-Woodhall**, won the long jump at the Summer Olympics!

The Paralympics' top medal winner was swimmer **Jiang Yuyan** of China, who won seven golds. Yuyan has just one arm and one leg but moves through the water so fast she is nicknamed the "Flying Fish." She won freestyle, butterfly, and backstroke events, as well as helped her country win two relays.

In all, nearly 100 world records were broken and more than 2.4 million tickets were sold, making this the second-most-popular Paralympics ever! Los Angeles will have big shoes to fill in 2028.

Masters was masterful in Paris!

TOP FIVE MEDAL STANDINGS

COUNTRY	G	S	B	TOTAL
1. China	94	76	50	220
2. Great Britain	49	44	31	124
3. United States	36	42	27	105
4. Brazil	25	26	38	89
5. Ukraine	22	28	32	82

American Heroes

Swimmer **Gia Pergolini** won the first gold for Team USA, speeding to victory in the 100-meter backstroke. She swims in races for people with visual issues and won a silver in the 50-meter freestyle as well!

Ezra Frech is one of the best high jumpers in the world, and he won that event. But in a huge surprise, he also won a 100-meter gold! Another American double winner, **Jaydin Blackwell**, won a 100, too, and set a world record to boot! He got a second gold plus another world record in a 400-meter run.

In badminton, **Jayci Simon** and **Miles Krajewski** won silver in doubles, the first medal in that sport for the United States in Olympic or Paralympic history!

Wheelchair rugby star **Chuck Aoki** won his fourth career medal, the most ever in his sport. He led the US team to a silver medal in this action-packed sport. He was joined on the coed team by **Sarah Adam**, making her the first US woman to medal in this sport.

The paratriathlon is a very tough event, combining swimming, cycling, and running.

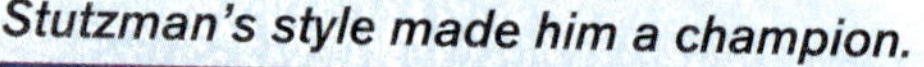

Stutzman's style made him a champion.

Krajewski and Simon were golden!

There were 12 different races for various abilities. Americans came home with eight medals in the races, including a record three golds. Congrats to winners **Hailey Danz**, **Chris Hammer**, and **Grace Norman**!

Swimmers **Ellie Marks** and **Christie Raleigh Crossley** won five medals each, the most among US athletes. Marks was chosen to carry the American flag in the Closing Ceremony!

The US men's wheelchair basketball team won gold for the third Paralympics in a row. US women grabbed a silver medal, its first since 1992.

Matt Stutzman does not have arms, but that did not stop him from winning gold in an archery event. Stutzman holds the bow with his foot, with the arrow released from a special clip at his shoulder. His opponent had both arms.

Record Setters

World records fell like bowling pins all over the Paris Paralympics!

- In a women's 1500-meter run, **Yayesh Gate Tesfaw** from Ethiopia set a world record that topped the previous mark by 10 seconds.
- Flying metal! Brazil's **Claudiney Batista dos Santos** held the discus record but set a new one to win gold. **Bobirjon Omonov** of Uzbekistan did the same in shot put.
- Australia's **James Turner** hasn't let having cerebral palsy (a nerve and brain disease) slow him down. He set a world record while winning gold in a 400-meter track race.
- Great Britain's **Poppy Maskill** had a great first-ever Paralympic swimming race. She set a world record in a 100-meter butterfly event. (Was it a lucky charm? Maskill's roommate, **Maisie Summers-Newton**, held Maskill's medal that night and then won her own gold!)

Oluwafemiayo celebrates her world record.

- Powerlifter **Folashade Oluwafemiayo** lifted 167 kg (368 pounds) to set a world record and won gold for Nigeria.
- Cycling track events had 11 new world records, including China's **Li Zhangyu** knocking four seconds off the 3000-meter individual pursuit mark.

Zakia Khudadadi

- Turkey's **Öznur Cüre Girdi** notched 704 points in an archery event, the first woman to go over 700 points in a Paralympics.
- Paraylympic firsts: Nepal's **Palesha Goverdhan** won a bronze medal in taekwondo, while **Zakia Khudadadi** earned a medal for the Refugee Paralympic Team.

STRAUSS

MLB

MAGIC MOMENT
With this mighty swing, Dodgers 1B Freddie Freeman got the 2024 World Series off to a great start (for LA!). He hit the first walk-off grand slam in World Series history, giving the Dodgers a 6-2 win in Game 1. They went on to win their eighth MLB championship in five games over the New York Yankees. The series capped off a record-setting MLB season—read on for all the highlights!

MLB 2024

In 2024, baseball fans, as usual, saw many brand-new things. The sport has such a long history, you'd think we'd seen it all before. But the game just keeps showing us that there is more to discover. The '24 season included the first member of a new club, a new low for losses, a slugger that nearly matched **Babe Ruth**, a historic rookie pitcher, and some surprise playoff teams.

The biggest story all summer was watching **Shohei Ohtani** make history. The Los Angeles Dodgers DH (he's also a pitcher when not injured) thrilled fans around the world by becoming the first player to hit 50 homers and steal 50 bases in one season! In the American League, the New York Yankees' **Aaron Judge** smacked 58 homers. His slugging numbers for the season were matched only by the great Ruth more than 100 years ago! And Pittsburgh pitcher **Paul Skenes** threw 17 pitches faster than 100 miles per hour in his first game . . . and just got better from there!

In other pitching news, two hurlers won their league's pitching Triple Crown (leading the league in wins, strikeouts, and ERA). Atlanta's **Chris Sale** had not won 10 games since 2018 but bounced back to All-Star form with 18 wins and a 2.38 ERA. In the AL, Detroit's **Tarik Skubal** shocked everyone by dominating. In his fifth season, he had his first winning record, plus he led the league with 18 wins and a 2.39 ERA. Wow!

On the flip side, the Chicago White Sox lost 121 games, the most by any team since 1900.

Tarik Skubal

A bounceback season from the Kansas City Royals was another big story. They lost 106 games in 2023 but made the playoffs in 2024, thanks to SS **Bobby Witt Jr.**'s record season. He was the first shortstop with two seasons of 30 home runs and 30 stolen bases!

Kansas City's Witt Jr. added a Gold Glove Award for defense to his awesome season.

The Detroit Tigers bounced back, too. They lost 84 games in 2023 and were 10 games out of a playoff spot in August. But with 39 wins in the last two months (the most in MLB), they made the playoffs for the first time in 10 seasons.

Two teams clinched their playoff spots with dramatic endings. With Ohtani on deck and the bases loaded, the Padres turned a game-ending triple play against the Dodgers. The win gave San Diego a wild card playoff spot. Then, when weather moved the final two games of the season to the Monday after everyone else had finished, the Braves and Mets faced off in a doubleheader. Both teams needed a win to clinch, and that's what they got. But the drama came in the first game when both teams stormed back late with dramatic drives. The capper was **Francisco Lindor**'s two-run homer in the ninth for the Mets win.

With so much news and excitement in the regular season, could the playoffs do the same? Read on to find out!

2024 FINAL MLB STANDINGS

AL EAST		AL CENTRAL		AL WEST	
Yankees	94–68	Guardians	92–69	Astros	88–73
Orioles	91–71	Royals	86–76	Mariners	85–77
Red Sox	81–81	Tigers	86–76	Rangers	78–84
Rays	80–82	Twins	82–80	Athletics	69–93
Blue Jays	74–88	White Sox	41–121	Angels	63–99

NL EAST		NL CENTRAL		NL WEST	
Phillies	95–67	Brewers	93–69	Dodgers	98–64
Braves	89–73	Cardinals	83–79	Padres	93–69
Mets	89–73	Cubs	83–79	Diamondbacks	89–73
Nationals	71–91	Reds	77–85	Giants	80–82
Marlins	62–100	Pirates	76–86	Rockies	61–101

Diamond Notes 2024

De La Cruz Cruises:

Reds SS **Elly De La Cruz** carried on from his breakout 2023 season. In April, he became the first player ever to have at least 8 homers and 17 steals in a single month! Over his first 198 games in the majors, he had 84 stolen bases, 80 extra-base hits, and 83 walks. He was the first player since 1900 to reach those totals that fast. He wound up leading MLB with 67 steals, and he had a career-best 25 homers. Unfortunately, he also led MLB with 218 strikeouts. De La Cruz is the first player ever to be tops in stolen bases and strikeouts!

De La Cruz takes a breather after another steal.

Hot Dogs from Heaven:

That's what the Seattle Mariners called their sky-high tasty treat. At several games, the team tossed hot dogs into the stands from the upper decks. But the doggies had help on the way down—mini-parachutes! Fans jumped up to snag a free meal after watching the wrapped dogs float down.

Phab Philly:

Philadelphia's **Ranger Suárez** was the first pitcher to start 9–0 with an ERA under 1.50 since **Juan Marichal** in 1966! The young lefty was a key part of the Phillies' historic 36–14 start, the best by a team since 2001 and the most wins in the first 50 games by a Phillies team. But Suárez later slumped to 12–8. The Phillies made the playoffs but lost in the Division Series.

The Judge Rules!:

Aaron Judge of the Yankees had a May to remember. He clubbed 14 homers as part of his 26 extra-base hits, one of the highest single-month totals in team history. He also was only the second Yankee ever with 30 extra-base hits in 30 games! Judge never stopped slugging, leading MLB with 58 homers, 144 RBI, and a .701 slugging average.

Hail, Grimace!:

The giant purple blob known as **Grimace** (right; a mascot of a certain famous chain of fast-food restaurants) threw out the first pitch at a Mets game June 12. The Mets then won seven games in a row and 12 of 14. Maybe he should pitch more often! Fans wore Grimace costumes to many games as the Mets made it all the way to the NLCS. Slugger **Pete Alonso** even wore purple cleats to thank Grimace for the good luck!

Speed Demons:

As every batter will tell you, pitchers are getting faster and faster. Two examples: On August 3, Angels pitcher **Ben Joyce** threw a pitch measured at 104.7 miles per hour—the fastest pitch recorded since Statcast began in 2008. Just four days later, veteran **Aroldis Chapman** of the Pittsburgh Pirates topped him at 105.1! Joyce kept the needle moving up. In September, he hit 105.5! The two are the only pitchers to top 105 . . . so far!

Great Start!:

Pittsburgh rookie pitcher **Paul Skenes** lit up radar guns in 2024. He had an ERA under 2.00 (1.99) and at least 150 Ks (167) in the first 22 games he started. No pitcher since 1900 had done that! He also started the All-Star Game for the NL after starting 6–0.

Skenes had a fantastic rookie season.

Two Teams—One Game:

How can a player play for both teams in the same game? This very rare baseball oddity happened in August to **Danny Jansen**. In June, he was a catcher for the Toronto Blue Jays in a game against the Boston Red Sox. The game was stopped due to rain. In July, Jansen was traded to Boston. In August, the rain game was completed . . . so the Red Sox put Jansen in their lineup to make history. He ended up being the catcher for an at-bat in which he had started out as the batter!

Diamond Notes
CONTINUED

Duran was Mr. Everything for Boston.

Wow!: Here are a few things MLB players did that just made us cheer!

- Texas OF **Wyatt Langford** was the first player ever to have a grand slam, an inside-the-park homer, and hit for the cycle in his rookie season.
- How many gloves does Minnesota's **Willi Castro** have? A lot! Castro played at least 25 games at five positions–SS, 2B, 3B, CF, LF. No one's ever done that before!
- The Padres' **Dylan Cease** allowed only 2 hits over three starts (including a July 25 no-hitter), the first time a pitcher had done that since 1901!
- Boston OF **Jarren Duran** checked all the boxes as the first player to get at least 10 triples, 20 homers, 30 steals, and 40 doubles in a season!
- Kansas City's **Bobby Witt Jr.** put up his own amazing season—the first shortstop with 10 triples, 25 steals, 30 homers, and 40 doubles in a season.
- Yankees **Aaron Judge** and **Juan Soto** were the first teammates ever to each get at least 40 homers, 100 RBI, and 120 walks in a season.

History in Rickwood: In 2024, MLB added Negro Leagues stats to its official lists. That changed the top of some of those lists. The new leader in career batting average (.372) and slugging percentage (.718) is catcher **Josh Gibson**! **Oscar Charleston**'s .363 batting average is now fifth all-time, too. The Negro Leagues played from 1920 to the 1950s because, until 1947, Black players were not allowed in MLB due to racist rules.

In honor of the history-making stats, MLB played a game at Rickwood Field in Birmingham, Alabama, the long-ago home of the Negro Leagues' Black Barons team. After former Negro Leagues players were honored on the field, the Cardinals and Giants faced off. St. Louis won 6-5.

Negro Leaguer Bill Greason throws the first pitch.

All About Ohtani

No player ever had a season like LA Dodgers DH **Shohei Ohtani** had in 2024.

Already a two-time MVP with the Angels, the star from Japan signed a 10-year, $700-million contract to move to the Dodgers. He paid off right away. Although he could not pitch while recovering from surgery, he was named the NL MVP for his offense alone. He took the mound again in 2025.

Ohtani became the first player in MLB history to hit 50 homers and steal 50 bases in the same season. His final totals of 54 homers and 59 steals were also the highest totals of his amazing career . . . so far!

Most people thought they had seen all Ohtani could do, but his game on September 19 amazed even his most loyal fans. In the Dodgers' 20-4 win over the Miami Marlins, he hit his 50th homer and stole his 50th base. In all, he went 6-for-6 with 3 homers, 10 RBI, and 2 steals. It was probably the best batting day a player has ever had!

Here are some of Ohtani's final regular-season stats, all tops in the NL:

- 54 home runs
- 130 runs batted in
- .390 on-base percentage
- .646 slugging average
- 411 total bases (also best in MLB)

And Ohtani was not done! In the playoffs, at one point he was 17-for-20 with runners in scoring position, Though injured for most of the World Series, he ended up with 14 runs and 14 hits in the postseason, including 3 homers and 10 RBI. At the Dodgers' World Series victory parade, he said (in English, a language he's still learning), "I'm so honored to be here and be part of this team." Trust us, Shohei . . . the honor is baseball's!

MLB Playoffs

WILD CARD PLAYOFFS

Tigers 2, Astros 0: Underdog Detroit swept two games to send Houston home.
Royals 2, Orioles 0: Another upset, as the Royals swept the favored O's. KC's Bobby Witt Jr. had both game-winning RBI.
Padres 2, Braves 0: Slugging OF Fernando Tatis Jr. led the way in his team's two-game sweep.
Mets 2, Brewers 1: Pete Alonso's ninth-inning three-run homer gave the Mets a come-from-behind 4-2 win in Game 3.

ALDS

Guardians 3, Tigers 2

Cleveland smoked the Tigers 7-0 in Game 1, but **Kerry Carpenter**'s dramatic ninth-inning homer gave Detroit a 3-0 win in Game 2. Detroit won Game 3 by the same score, as six Tigers pitchers shut out Cleveland. **David Fry**'s 3 RBI led Cleveland to a series-tying 5-3 win. In Game 5, **Lane Thomas** smacked a grand slam that sent Guardians to the next round 7-3.

Fry's homer helped Cleveland win Game 3.

Yankees 3, Royals 1

Gleyber Torres and **Austin Wells** had 2 RBI each to lead New York to a 6-5 Game 1 win. In Game 2, the Royals scored four in the fourth and won 4-2. A homer by **Giancarlo Stanton** gave the Yanks a 3-2 win in Game 3. The Yankees won the series with a 3-1 win in Game 4 behind SP **Gerrit Cole**.

NLDS

Mets 3, Phillies 1

The Mets made a late rally to win Game 1 6-2. In Game 2, they came back again to tie the game, only to see the Phillies win 7-6 in the bottom of the ninth. The Mets won Game 3 behind a great start by **Sean Manaea**. In Game 4, a **Francisco Lindor** grand slam gave the series to the Mets with a 4-1 win.

Dodgers 3, Padres 2

Shohei Ohtani smacked a Game 1 three-run homer, and the Dodgers won a 7-5 slugfest. San Diego starter **Yu Darvish** shut down the Dodgers in Game 2, while the Padres tied an MLB playoff-game record with 6 homers and won 10-2. The Padres held on for a 6-5 win in Game 3. The Dodgers tied the series with an 8-0 Game 4 win. In the clinching Game 5,

Mets hero Lindor watches his slam fly.

Dodgers pitching shut out the Padres 2-0, while **Kiké Hernández** and **Teoscar Hernández** (no relation) both homered.

ALCS

Yankees 4, Guardians 1

Homers by Stanton and **Juan Soto** were part of the Yankees' 5-2 win in Game 1. Judge had 3 RBI to lead New York to a 6-3 win in Game 2. Game 3 was a thriller. **Aaron Judge**'s homer tied the game in the top of the eighth, then Stanton's put the Yanks ahead. But Cleveland tied it with a bottom-of-the-ninth shot from **Jhonkensy Noel** and won it 7-5 on Fry's walk-off homer in the tenth. Cleveland rallied from four runs down to tie Game 4 at 6-6, but New York scored two in the ninth to win Game 4 8-6. In Game 5, the Yankees earned their 41st trip to the World Series when Soto smacked a three-run homer in the tenth inning, leading to a 5-2 win.

NLCS

Dodgers 4, Mets 2

Jack Flaherty of the Dodgers led his team to a third straight shutout in the playoffs. **Mookie Betts** had a three-run double, while Ohtani had 2 hits and an RBI in LA's 9-hit attack. The Mets bounced back with a 7-3 win, led by **Mark Vientos**' grand slam. Ohtani had a three-run homer to highlight LA's 8-0 win in Game 3. Ohtani hit another homer to lead off Game 4, and the Dodgers piled on lots more to win 10-2. **Pete Alonso** and **Starling Marte** each had 3 RBI to lead the Mets' big offensive show in a 12-6 Game 5 win. The Dodgers headed to their 22nd World Series by winning Game 6 10-5, as **Will Smith**'s three-run homer led another big game for the bats.

Ohtani led off Game 4 with a homer.

World Series

In 2024, the Dodgers and Yankees faced off for the title for the 12th time. No two teams have met as often in the World Series. It was the epic battle baseball fans were waiting for!

GAME 1 Dodgers 6, Yankees 3

Game 1 ended with the first grand slam walk-off homer in World Series history! Both starting pitchers were great, with **Gerrit Cole** and **Jack Flaherty** mostly shutting down powerful offensive teams. **Giancarlo Stanton**'s homer gave the Yankees a 2-1 lead in the sixth. A **Shohei Ohtani** double and a **Mookie Betts** single tied the game, which went to extra innings. In the top of the tenth, the Yankees pushed across a go-ahead run. Then came the drama. The Dodgers got a walk, a single, and an intentional walk to Ohtani. **Freddie Freeman**, dealing with an injured ankle, limped up and smacked a towering homer that sent Dodger Stadium into a huge celebration.

GAME 2 Dodgers 4, Yankees 2

Freeman homered again, and the Dodgers got great starting pitching . . . again. **Yoshinobu Yamamoto** went 6.1 shutout innings and gave up only 1 hit. The Dodgers also got homers from **Tommy Edman** and **Teoscar Hernández**. They had to survive a ninth-inning rally by the Yankees and got a scare when Ohtani injured his shoulder stealing a base . . . but he rallied to keep playing in the series.

Freeman's happy teammates met him at home in Game 1.

GAME 3 Dodgers 4, Yankees 2

Freeman homered . . . of course! His two-run shot got the Dodgers going in the first inning, and they held on to win. Betts and **Kiké Hernández** each knocked in runs as well. Starter

Walker Buehler picked up where Yamamoto left off, throwing five scoreless innings. The Dodgers also got great defense. In the fourth inning, LF Teoscar Hernández threw out Stanton at the plate to keep the Yankees from scoring. Betts later made a diving catch, and SS Edman made a big stretch to get a key out at second base. After New York's **Alex Verdugo** hit a two-run homer in the bottom of the ninth, Edman made another nice play on the game's final out.

GAME 4 Yankees 11, Dodgers 4

Freeman homered . . . again (wow!), but it was not enough, and the Yankees avoided a sweep. Their big hit was a grand slam of their own. SS **Anthony Volpe** cleared the bases in the third to give the Yankees a 5-2 lead. After adding another run, the Yanks put up five in the eighth inning to seal the win. The Dodgers' "bullpen" game didn't work, with its four relievers allowing 11 runs, 9 hits, 6 walks, and a hit batter.

GAME 5 Dodgers 7, Yankees 6

The Dodgers won their eighth World Series title with the biggest comeback ever in a series-clinching game! New York went up 5-0, thanks to homers from Judge, Stanton, and **Jazz Chisholm Jr.** But then in the fifth, they collapsed. Judge made an error, and then Volpe did, too. The Dodgers took advantage with clutch hits to tie the game 5-5. Freeman had a key hit (a two-out, two-run single), while Teoscar Hernández knocked a double for two more runs. The Yankees went ahead in the sixth, but LA stormed back. In the eighth, they loaded the bases and got sacrifice flies from **Gavin Lux** and Betts for the tying and winning runs. Game 3 starter Buehler came in to close out the game in the ninth and start the celebration! Freeman was named the MVP after hitting 4 homers and tying an all-time World Series record with 12 RBI.

2024 Award Winners

Aaron Judge

MOST VALUABLE PLAYER

AL Aaron Judge, Yankees

NL Shohei Ohtani, Dodgers

CY YOUNG AWARD

AL Tarik Skubal, Tigers

NL Chris Sale, Braves

ROOKIE OF THE YEAR

AL Luis Gil, Yankees

NL Paul Skenes, Pirates

HANK AARON AWARD

AL Aaron Judge, Yankees

NL Shohei Ohtani, Dodgers

MANAGER OF THE YEAR

AL Stephen Vogt, Guardians

NL Pat Murphy, Brewers

ROBERTO CLEMENTE AWARD (COMMUNITY SERVICE)

Salvador Perez, Royals

2024 Stat Champs

Ryan Helsley

AL Hitting Leaders

.332 BATTING AVERAGE
Bobby Witt Jr., Royals

58 HOME RUNS
144 RBI
Aaron Judge, Yankees

44 STOLEN BASES
José Caballero, Rays

NL Hitting Leaders

.314 AVERAGE
Luis Arráez, Padres

54 HOME RUNS
130 RBI
Shohei Ohtani, Dodgers

67 STOLEN BASES
Elly De La Cruz, Reds

AL Pitching Leaders

18 WINS
228 STRIKEOUTS
2.39 ERA
Tarik Skubal, Tigers

47 SAVES
Emmanuel Clase, Guardians

NL Pitching Leaders

18 WINS
225 STRIKEOUTS
2.38 ERA
Chris Sale, Braves

49 SAVES
Ryan Helsley, Cardinals

College Softball

FINAL EIGHT

After eight teams made it to the Women's College World Series, two teams from Texas met in the championship series.

Florida	Tennessee
Mississippi	Texas
Oklahoma	Texas Tech
Oregon	UCLA

GAME 1 Texas 2, Texas Tech 1

Tech was in charge in this one behind the awesome pitching of star **NiJaree Canady**. But in the sixth inning, ahead 1-0, Canady tried to walk **Reese Atwood** on purpose. But one of the pitches was too close, so Atwood smacked a two-run single for the winning runs.

GAME 2 Texas Tech 4, Texas 3

Canady was great again, and the Tech offense came through behind her to force a Game 3. Two runs in the sixth inning were the difference after Texas scored two in the final inning before Canady struck out **Kayden Henry** to end the game.

GAME 3 Texas 10, Texas Tech 4

The clinching game was pretty much over early. Texas scored five runs in the first inning, all off of Canady. The big hit was a three-run home run by **Leighann Goode**. Canady finally ran out of gas after throwing every other pitch for Tech in the World Series.

Goode's teammate **Mia Scott** did her one better, crushing a grand slam that ran the score to 10-0. Tech rallied with three in the fifth and another run late, but they were not enough. The Longhorns danced on the field with the first NCAA championship trophy in this sport in school history. On the mound, **Teagan Kavan** was great. She pitched more than 31 innings at the World Series and did not allow a single earned run. That was enough for her to earn the Most Outstanding Player award.

Kagan was lights-out for Texas.

Dogpile! LSU jumps for joy after winning the Men's College World Series.

College Baseball

FINAL EIGHT

Eight teams, highlighted by surprise entry Murray State, headed to Omaha, Nebraska, for the 78th Men's College World Series. The championship final matched LSU and Coastal Carolina.

Arkansas	LSU
Arizona	Oregon State
Coastal Carolina	UCLA
Louisville	Murray State

GAME 1 LSU 1, Coastal Carolina 0

Tigers ace **Kade Anderson** threw a gem, a shutout with 10 strikeouts. LSU scored its only run in the first inning thanks to an RBI single from **Steven Milam**. Anderson shut down the Chanticleers the rest of the way. Zero after zero hit the scoreboard. It was the first loss by Coastal Carolina in 26 games!

GAME 2 LSU 5, Coastal Carolina 3

The Tigers earned their second college championship in three seasons with a solid win. A pair of two-RBI singles in the fourth inning from **Chris Stanfield** and **Derek Curiel** proved to be the big hits, breaking up a 1-1 tie. Starter **Anthony Eyanson** was nearly as good as teammate Anderson. The win gave LSU its eighth national championship, the second-most ever.

What a Game!

During the playoffs before to the final series, Arkansas pitcher **Gage Wood** had a game for the ages. He threw a no-hitter with 19 strikeouts, a single-game MCWS record. He missed a perfect game by just one walk. Wood's team beat Murray State 3-0. It was just the third MCWS no-no ever.

ALL TOGETHER NOW!
The Philadelphia Eagles crowded around the Vince Lombardi Trophy after beating the Kansas City Chiefs 40-22 to win Super Bowl LIX (59). It was revenge for the Eagles, who had lost the big game to the Chiefs two seasons ago. For the complete story of the awesome and action-packed 2024 NFL season, turn the page!

NFL

NFL 2024

The NFL was packed with super stories and great players again in 2024. Some teams continued to be among the best, and several teams moved up this year to join them!

The Kansas City Chiefs came into the season as two-time Super Bowl champs. Then they rolled to the AFC's best record, with a twist. They won 15 games, but only scored 30 points in two of those wins of them! Thank you, defense!

Two NFC North teams had outstanding seasons. The Detroit Lions rode the NFL's best offense to a 15–2 record, scoring 40 or more points in six different games. They ended with an NFL-best 564 points. The Minnesota Vikings were right there with them at 14–3, led by superstar WR **Justin Jefferson** and a surprising season from QB **Sam Darnold**. It took a final-game Week 18 battle between these two teams to decide the No. 1 seed in the NFC (the Lions won it). A good season by Green Bay QB **Jordan Love** meant that the division had three playoff teams and was the only division with three teams with 11 or more wins.

In the West, both Los Angeles teams rallied from poor starts to make the playoffs. The Chargers were led by new coach **Jim Harbaugh** to an 11–6 record. The Rams reached the No. 3 seed after winning the NFC West. In the East, led by MVP candidate RB **Saquon Barkley** (see page 37), the Philadelphia Eagles began a return to the Super Bowl with a 14–3 season. Barkley finished just over 100 yards short of a single-season NFL rushing record. Another NFC East team earned a surprise playoff spot. Rookie QB **Jayden Daniels** had a great season while leading Washington to a 12–5 record.

A few teams fell short of their goals. The Dallas Cowboys had won 12 games in each of the past three seasons, but were only 7–10 in 2024. Injuries were a reason, but they also found other ways to lose over and over.

Ja'Marr Chase

A GREAT NFL MVP RACE!

In one of the closest votes in NFL MVP history, Buffalo QB **Josh Allen** (left) squeaked out a win over Baltimore QB **Lamar Jackson**. Philadelphia RB **Saquon Barkley** was third. The vote was also odd because Jackson was named first-team All-Pro ahead of Allen! Both players had great seasons, but there's only one trophy!

The San Francisco 49ers also had high hopes, coming off three straight winning seasons (and the 2023 NFC title). This season, their offense never clicked. An injury to key RB **Christian McCaffrey** didn't help.

The Cincinnati Bengals didn't make the playoffs, but star WR **Ja'Marr Chase** had an amazing season. He had a "triple crown," leading the NFL in catches, TD catches, and receiving yards.

A big story all season was who would win the NFL MVP. Buffalo Bills QB **Josh Allen** got off to a hot start and ended with 12 rushing TDs to go with 28 TDs through the air. Baltimore's **Lamar Jackson** became the first QB with 4,000 passing yards and 800 rushing yards; he also threw 41 TDs with only 4 picks. Barkley's chase of the NFL record put him into the mix as well.

Could a new team knock the Chiefs out of three-peating as Super Bowl champs? When the playoffs began, it looked like Kansas City was just one of several teams with the tools to win it all. Who got the Vince Lombardi Trophy? Read on to find out!

2024 Final Regular-Season Standings

AFC EAST		AFC NORTH		AFC SOUTH		AFC WEST	
Bills*	13–4	Ravens*	12–5	Texans*	10–7	Chiefs*	15–2
Dolphins	8–9	Steelers*	10–7	Colts	8–9	Chargers*	11–6
Jets	5–12	Bengals	9–8	Jaguars	4–13	Broncos*	10–7
Patriots	4–13	Browns	3–14	Titans	3–14	Raiders	4–13

NFC EAST		NFC NORTH		NFC SOUTH		NFC WEST	
Eagles*	14–3	Lions*	15–2	Buccaneers*	10–7	Rams*	10–7
Commanders*	12–5	Vikings*	14–3	Falcons	8–9	Seahawks	10–7
Cowboys	7–10	Packers*	11–6	Panthers	5–12	Cardinals	8–9
Giants	3–14	Bears	5–12	Saints	5–12	49ers	6–11

*Made Playoffs

Weeks 1-4

Kamara had a big day against Dallas.

WEEK 1

Playoff Repeat: In a 2023 NFC playoff game, the Lions beat the Rams 24-23. Their rematch to open the 2024 season was almost as close. Detroit needed a last-minute field goal and then a touchdown in overtime to beat LA 26-20, after the Rams had taken a fourth-quarter lead.

Bears Roar: Chicago trailed 17-3 at halftime to Tennessee, but rallied to win 24-17. They got a blocked-punt TD, 3 field goals, and a clutch pick-six by **Tyrique Stevenson** to clinch the big win. No. 1 draft pick QB **Caleb Williams** threw for only 93 yards . . . but he won!

Bounceback Bills: Buffalo almost fell in a big upset, but ended up beating Arizona 34-28. Bills QB **Josh Allen** threw 2 TD passes and ran for 2 scores. Buffalo's defense had to stop the Cardinals' final pass at the goal line to hold on for the win.

Patriots . . . Win?: New England was not expected to start the season with a W . . . but they did. RB **Rhamondre Stevenson** led the way with 120 rushing yards and a TD. The Bengals also made just too many mistakes, losing 16-10.

WEEK 2

Seven for Three: That math makes sense when you find out that Washington K **Austin Seibert** kicked 7 field goals to score all of his team's points in a 21-18 win over the Giants. The final FG, from 30 yards, came as the clock ran out!

Saints Alive!: RB **Alvin Kamara** had a monster day, scoring 4 TDs and running for 115 yards as the Saints stomped the Cowboys 44-19. QB **Derek Carr** threw 2 TD passes and scored on a run. New Orleans topped 40 points for the second straight week.

Pair of Upsets: It was a little early for upsets, but few experts thought these games would turn out like they did. The Ravens were leading the Raiders by 10 points, but Las Vegas scored a late game-winning field goal to win 26-23. Meanwhile, the Vikings surprised the 49ers, the defending NFC champs. WR **Justin Jefferson**'s 97-yard TD catch-and-run was the big play in a 23-17 upset.

TRIVIA TIME!

When the Commanders beat the Bengals 38-33 on a Monday night, it was the first NFL game since 1940 with *zero* punts and *zero* turnovers!

WEEK 3

Purple Power: The Minnesota Vikings continued a hot start by beating the Houston Texans 34-7. QB **Sam Darnold** tied a career high with 4 TD passes, including one to superstar **Jefferson**. The Texans have actually never beaten the Vikings!

Packer Power: When your defense makes 8 sacks and scores a pick-six, you just need the offense to keep pace. Backup QB **Malik Willis** did just that for Green Bay, running and passing for TDs to help his team beat Tennessee 30-14.

Comeback in LA: The Rams trailed by 14 points in the second half, but a long pass and a great punt return helped them rally to beat the 49ers 27-24. After a long **Matthew Stafford** pass to **Tutu Atwell**, **Kyren Williams** scored his third TD of the day to tie the score. A 38-yard punt return by **Xavier Smith** helped put the Rams in place for **Joshua Karty**'s winning field goal with just two seconds left.

WEEK 4

You Know Koo: After the Saints pulled ahead in the final minute, the Falcons rallied to set up **Younghoe Koo** for a long field goal. His 58-yarder set a career record and won the game 24-23.

Texans Terrific: With just 18 seconds left, Houston QB **C.J. Stroud** hit **Dare Ogunbowale** with a short pass that the receiver carried into the end zone for a late TD. The score gave the Texans a come-from-behind 24-20 win over the Jaguars, who were searching for their first win.

Flacco to the Rescue: After the Colts' QB **Anthony Richardson** was injured, veteran backup **Joe Flacco** stepped in. Good thing he was there! He threw 2 TD passes and led Indianapolis to a 27-24 win over the Steelers. It was Pittsburgh's first loss of the season.

Perfect Night: QB **Jared Goff** of the Lions was 18-for-18 (and even caught a TD pass) while leading Detroit to a 42-29 win over the Seahawks. Goff threw the most passes ever completed without a miss in one game . . . in NFL history!

Jared Goff

Weeks 5-8

WEEK 5

Falcons Fly!: QB **Kirk Cousins** set a personal and team record with 509 passing yards. His fourth TD pass came in overtime to **KhaDarel Hodge** for a wild 36-30 win over Tampa Bay. Atlanta had tied the game in the final seconds on a 52-yard field goal by **Younghoe Koo**.

Defense Day Off 1: The Cincinnati and Baltimore defenses took the afternoon off (just kidding). But the teams' offenses both had big days. Ravens QB **Lamar Jackson** threw 4 TD passes and ran for 55 yards. Cincinnati's **Joe Burrow** set a personal record with 5 TD passes, including one for 70 yards to **Ja'Marr Chase**. Ravens RB **Derrick Henry** had 92 rushing yards, including 51 on a play that set up **Justin Tucker**'s game-winning kick in overtime. The wild game ended up Baltimore 41, Cincinnati 38.

Distance Kick: The Houston Texans continued a great early-season run by surprising the Buffalo Bills. Second-year star QB **C.J. Stroud** continued to impress, throwing for 331 yards. He led his team on a late drive that ended with **Ka'imi Fairbairn** nailing a 59-yard field goal on the game's final play give Houston the 23-20 win.

WEEK 6

Defense Day Off 2: The Ravens and Commanders showed off two of the NFL's best offenses in a game that included almost 800 yards of total offense. Baltimore won 30-23. Rookie QB **Jayden Daniels** of the Commanders was good (269 passing yards and 2 TDs), but Baltimore had Henry. The veteran RB scored twice and ran for 132 yards.

Big Second Half: The Buccaneers trailed the Saints 27-24 at halftime. Good thing they play two halves! Tampa Bay scored 27 points in the second half to romp 51-27. Tampa QB **Baker Mayfield** had 4 TD passes and threw for 325 yards. The Saints were the first NFL team ever to score 27 points in one half and then zero in the second!

Caleb's Big Day: The Bears continued a winning streak thanks to 4 TD passes from rookie star **Caleb Williams**, including 2 to TE **Cole Kmet**. The 35-16 win over Jacksonville moved the Bears to a surprising 4–2.

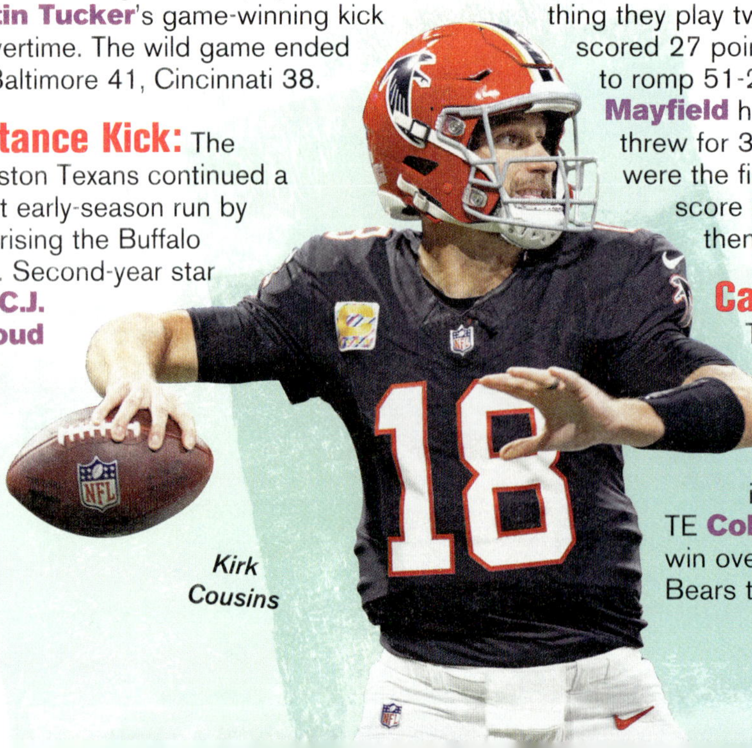

Kirk Cousins

Lions Lasso Cowboys: Detroit rolled into Dallas and crushed the Cowboys 47-9. **Jared Goff** had 3 TD passes for the Lions, while **David Montgomery** ran for two TDs. It was the biggest home defeat for Dallas since 1988!

Brown (right) caught this tipped pass for a game-winner!

WEEK 7

Vikings Vanquished!: Minnesota lost its first game of the season in a thriller to Detroit. The Vikings had the best rushing defense in the league, but the Lions ran all over them. RB **Jahmyr Gibbs** had 116 yards and a pair of TDs. Goff also threw 2 TDs. Detroit needed a field goal with 15 seconds left to win 31-29.

Welcome Home: **Saquon Barkley** was a star RB for the Giants for six seasons, but he moved to the Eagles for 2024. In his first game against his old team, he showed them what they were missing. Barkley ran for 176 yards and a TD, driving Philadelphia to a 28-3 win.

Russell's Return: After missing the Steelers' first six games with an injury, QB **Russell Wilson** returned in style. He threw for 264 yards and 2 TD passes, plus he ran for another score. He kickstarted the Pittsburgh offense, and they beat the Jets 37-15. The Pittsburgh D helped by intercepting two **Aaron Rodgers** passes.

Still Perfect: The Chiefs became the last undefeated team left after beating the 49ers 28-18. QB **Patrick Mahomes** went without a TD pass for the second straight game. But he had a rushing TD, one of 4 by the Chiefs, including 2 by **Kareem Hunt**. The defense also chipped in with 3 interceptions.

Bounce Back: Baltimore lost the first two games of the season, then ripped off a five-game winning streak. Win No. 5 was an impressive 41-31 defeat of Tampa Bay. Jackson lit up the scoreboard for Baltimore with 5 TD passes, including 2 to TE **Mark Andrews**.

WEEK 8

Miracle Ending!: Washington's Jayden Daniels was already having a great season. But on October 27, the rookie QB added a big highlight. On the final play of the game against the Bears, Daniels scrambled 40 yards back and forth behind the line of scrimmage before heaving a pass 65 yards in the air! The ball was tipped and then landed in the hands of **Noah Brown** in the end zone. Touchdown! Game-winner! Miracle play! The Commanders celebrated a surprise 18-15 win.

Big-time Backup: When Browns QB **Deshaun Watson** was hurt, Cleveland fans feared the worst. But veteran backup **Jameis Winston** had a surprise. He threw for 334 yards and 3 TD passes to lead his team to a 29-24 upset of the Ravens.

Weeks 9–12

WEEK 9

Long Wait: After losing six straight games as the Panthers' starter, QB **Bryce Young** finally got a win. RB **Chuba Hubbard** had two TDs to help Carolina knock off New Orleans 23-22.

Big Bad Burrow: Bengals QB **Joe Burrow** had a huge day, tying a career record with 5 TD passes. Two of them went to TE **Mike Gesicki**. RB **Chase Brown** had the best game of his young career, rushing for 120 yards. It all added up to a 41-24 win over the Raiders.

Heckuva Half: Buffalo and Miami traded the lead three times in a wild second half that included 3 TD passes by Buffalo QB **Josh Allen** and 2 Miami TDs. It all came down to a 61-yard field goal try by Buffalo's **Tyler Bass** . . . it was good! Buffalo won 30-27.

Video Game Move: **Saquon Barkley** was the big story in his Eagles' 28-23 win over the Jaguars. Barkley had a rushing TD and caught a TD pass. He also had 159 rushing yards. Some of them came after he made an incredible *backward* leap over a tackler! Instant highlight!

Barkley jumped backward over the Jags!

WEEK 10

Thursday Special: The Ravens and Bengals got Week 10 off to a big start, combining for 69 points, 711 passing yards, and 8 TD passes. Cincy's **Ja'Marr Chase** had a lot of them—3 TDs for 264 receiving yards, including TD catches for 67 and 70 yards. Ravens QB **Lamar Jackson** led a second-half comeback that included 21 points in the fourth quarter. The Bengals got within one with less than a minute left. They went for two to try to win, but the pass was broken up. Baltimore won a wild game 35-34.

Still Lucky: The Chiefs went to 9–0 with another comeback win. All but two of the team's wins to this point had been by one score or less! They found a new way to wriggle into a W when they blocked a last-play field goal and held on to beat Denver 16-14.

Don't Throw Picks!: That's one of the key rules for quarterbacks. Throw interceptions, and your team probably loses. Not this weekend! Detroit's **Jared Goff** threw a career-high 5 picks, but the Lions rallied to beat the Texans 26-23. **Jake Bates** kicked a game-winning 52-yard field goal. Meanwhile, the Vikings' **Sam Darnold** threw 3 interceptions . . . and the Vikes held on to beat the Jaguars 12-7.

WEEK 11

Double Trouble: In the fourth quarter of a tight NFC East game, Barkley sealed the deal. First, he scored on a 23-yard run. After the Eagles picked off a Washington pass, he scored on a 39-yard run. Two TDs in less than 30 seconds of game time! It added up to a 26-18 Eagles win.

Who Needs TDs?: Not the Steelers! For the second time this season (tying an NFL record), Pittsburgh won a game without scoring a TD. **Chris Boswell** kicked 6 field goals (including 3 over 50 yards!). Pittsburgh knocked off division rival Baltimore 18-16.

No More Undefeateds: Buffalo handed Kansas City its first loss of the season. Allen capped the game with a 26-yard TD run with just over two minutes left to make the final score 30-21. **James Cook** had 2 rushing TDs for the Bills.

Late Drama: The Chargers moved to 7–3 under new coach **Jim Harbaugh**. They had to hold on after giving up a 21-point lead to the Bengals. But the Cincinnati kicker missed 2 field goals. With 18 seconds left in a tie game, **J.K. Dobbins** raced 29 yards for the final score in a 34-27 Chargers win.

WEEK 12

Snow Problem: The Cleveland Browns didn't let a little snow (okay, a *lot* of snow!) get in their way of a 24-19 upset of the Steelers. Cleveland led 18-6, but the Steelers forged ahead. Then, with less than two minutes left, Browns RB **Nick Chubb** stomped through the snow to score the winning TD. Browns players made snow angels in the end zone to celebrate!

Titans Top Texans: Tennessee pulled off an upset by beating the Texans 32-27. The big play was a 70-yard TD throw from **Will Levis** to **Chig Okonkwo** in the fourth quarter. Houston nearly tied the game after that, but missed a field goal.

Are They the Best?: Detroit rolled to a 24-6 win over the Indianapolis Colts, becoming the first NFC team with 10 wins in 2024. The power-running team of **Jahmyr Gibbs** (2 TDs) and **David Montgomery** (1 TD) led the way. It was the first time the Lions were 10–1 since way back in 1934!

Cleveland's Ogbo Okoronkwo was a snow angel!

Allen set an NFL record with this TD run, but his Bills were upset by the Rams.

Weeks 13–15

WEEK 13

Mr. Everything: Buffalo **Josh Allen** became the first QB ever to pass, run, and catch a TD in the same game! His Bills beat the Niners 35-10 in a game played in heavy snow. Allen's receiving TD was a classic. **Amari Cooper** caught a short pass near the goal line. The Niners D stood him up, but Allen was coming in from behind. Cooper tossed the ball back to Allen, who dove into the end zone!

Wild Night in Denver: Cleveland's **Jameis Winston** threw for a team-record 497 yards. WR **Jerry Jeudy**, a former Bronco, had a career-best 235 yards on 9 catches. So the Browns won, right? Nope. Winston also threw pick-sixes that Denver returned for 44 and 71 yards. Broncos QB **Bo Nix** rallied his team for a go-ahead fourth-quarter field goal in their 41-32 Monday night win.

Another Squeaker: For the eighth time this season, the Chiefs won by 7 points or fewer. How long could they keep up this "lucky" streak? This win came thanks to Raiders' mistakes. Las Vegas was just about to kick what would have been a game-winning field goal. But they were called for a penalty and then fumbled! The Chiefs held on to win 19-17.

WEEK 14

Good Calls: Lions coach **Dan Campbell** chose to go for it on fourth down five times . . . and most of them paid off. The last one set up a game-winning field goal as Detroit beat Green Bay 34-31. **Jared Goff** had 2 TD passes (both on fourth down!) as the Lions set a new team record with their 11th win in a row.

Ram Tough: Allen went into the NFL history books again. He was the first player ever with 3 passing TDs and 3 rushing TDs in one game. His fantasy-football-perfect day was not enough for the win, however. Rams QB **Matthew Stafford** threw 2 TDs, and LA used a key blocked-punt TD to edge Buffalo 44-42.

Fantastic Fourth: Minnesota and Atlanta were tied as the fourth quarter began. Then the Vikings piled on 3 TDs to end with a 42-21 win. **Sam Darnold** threw 5 TD passes in the game, 3 to **Jordan Addison** and 2 to megastar **Justin Jefferson**.

WEEK 15

Defense Day Off: In what some fans were calling a Super Bowl preview, Buffalo and Detroit showed off their awesome offenses in an exciting 48-42 Bills win. Detroit's Goff became the first QB ever to throw for 400 yards and 5 TDs and no interceptions . . . and lose the game! Allen continued his hot streak, rushing for 2 scores and passing for 2 more. The loss snapped Detroit's 11-game win streak.

Rule Number One: Colts RB **Jonathan Taylor** learned a painful lesson when his team lost 31-13 to the Broncos. At the end of a 41-yard run toward the end zone, Taylor let the ball fall out of his hand *before* he crossed the goal line. He just dropped it in a too-early celebration. Denver's D forced 5 turnovers and scored a big TD, too.

Bucs' Big Day: Tampa Bay kept its shot at a playoff alive with a 40-17 win over the Chargers. QB **Baker Mayfield** had 4 TD passes, 2 to superstar **Mike Evans**. Chargers QB **Justin Herbert** threw his first interception in 357 attempts!

Who Needs Touchdowns?: The rain was pouring down as the 49ers hosted the Rams. It was hard to pass and hard to run. Bring on the kickers! The Rams' **Joshua Karty** made 4 field goals, while SF's **Jake Moody** made 2 as the Rams won 12-6.

Big Stop!: On the game's final play, the Saints scored to pull within one point of the Commanders. New Orleans decided to go for two points and the win, but Washington stopped them! The 20-19 win kept the Commanders' playoff hopes alive.

Mike Evans

Weeks 16–18

Dicker the kicker scored on a rare play.

Oops!: Tampa Bay had a chance to clinch a playoff spot with a win in Dallas. It didn't work out, and Dallas won 26-24. The Cowboys' **Jourdan Lewis** snagged a TD pass out of the hands of a Tampa receiver for a key interception. Then Dallas forced a fumble as the Bucs were driving toward a possible winning FG. Dallas K **Brandon Aubrey** was a star, nailing 4 FGs, including 3 of 50 yards or more.

Tied at the Top: Baltimore beat Pittsburgh 34-17 to create a tie in the AFC North with just two games left. QB **Lamar Jackson** had 3 TD passes for the Ravens. **Marlon Humphrey** scored on a pick-six to clinch the big win and a playoff spot. Jackson had 2 TD passes, taking him to 37 on the season, a new Ravens team record.

WEEK 16

Know the Rules: NFL football has a lot of tiny and rarely seen rules. One of these helped the Chargers win a big game. When a punt returner makes a fair catch, his team can choose to try a free kick as a field goal instead of running a play. **Cameron Dicker** of the Chargers did just that, making a 57-yard field goal as the first half ended. It was the first free-kick FG in 48 years! The points helped LA rally to beat Denver 34-27.

Rookie Star: Atlanta handed first-round draft pick QB **Michael Penix Jr.** the starting job for this game. He came through big-time! Penix guided his team to a 34-7 win over the Giants. He got a lot of help from the Falcons' defense, which returned 2 interceptions for TDs.

WEEK 17

NFL Best: On Christmas Day, Jackson topped **Michael Vick** to become the top rushing QB in NFL history (he ended the season with 6,173 yards). Even better, Jackson led his Ravens to a big 31-2 win over Houston, cementing Baltimore's spot in the playoffs. RB **Derrick Henry** continued his great season, rushing for 147 yards and a TD.

Rookie Bests: The Raiders won't make the playoffs in 2024, but they made some news in a 25-10 win over the Saints. **Brock Bowers** set a new record for receiving yards by a rookie tight end; he finished the season with 1,194 yards. He also reached 108 catches on the season (he ended the year with 112). That's a new record for any rookie receiver, topping a 2023 mark by **Puka Nacua** of the Rams.

Big Day in Philly: The Eagles clinched the NFC East with a 41-7 defeat of division-rival Dallas. With 167 rushing yards, RB **Saquon Barkley** became the ninth player ever to top 2,000 in a season. The Eagles managed to win behind their third-string QB, **Tanner McKee**, who had 2 TD passes after coming in late when **Jalen Hurts** was injured.

Playoff Power: Both Los Angeles teams, the Rams and the Chargers, won games that clinched playoff spots in Week 17. The Rams squeaked past the Cardinals 13-9. It was a big comeback after starting the season 1–4. The Chargers had less trouble, crushing the Patriots 40-7. QB **Justin Herbert** had 3 TD passes, and the team earned a playoff spot for the first time since 2018.

Commanders Are In!: Washington clinched its first playoff spot since 2020 with a 30-24 overtime win over the Falcons. With 3 TD passes, star rookie QB **Jayden Daniels** led the way. He became the all-time rookie leader in rushing yards by a QB. By the end of the season, Washington had won eight more games than it did in 2023.

WEEK 18

MVP Worthy: Baltimore clinched the AFC North title as Jackson led his Ravens to a 35-10 win over the Browns. Along the way, Jackson became the first QB to pass for more than 4,000 yards and rush for more than 800 yards in the same season. He finished the season with 41 TD passes and only 4 interceptions!

Lamar Jackson

Bucs Clinch: Tampa Bay came from behind to beat New Orleans and win the NFC South. **Baker Mayfield** threw 2 TDs and ran for a career-high 68 yards. Tampa Bay WR **Mike Evans** reached 1,000 receiving yards for the 11th season in a row, tying the great **Jerry Rice**.

Big Bad Bo: Okay, yes, the Chiefs hardly played any regulars . . . but the Broncos had to beat whomever Kansas City sent out. And they did, winning 38-0 to earn Denver's first playoff spot since way back in 2015! Rookie QB **Bo Nix** continued his great season, passing for 4 TDs and 321 yards.

Lions No. 1: For the first time in NFL history, two teams with 13 (or more) wins met in the regular season. Detroit (14–2) beat Minnesota (14–2) behind **Jahmyr Gibbs**' 4 TDs (3 rushing, 1 receiving). The Lions defense played very well, twice stopping the Vikes on fourth-and-goal. The 31-9 win gave Detroit a week off, too!

Wild Card Weekend

AFC

Texans 32, Chargers 12

LA QB **Justin Herbert** had thrown only 3 interceptions in 2024. In this game, the Texans picked him off four times, returning one for a pick-six. Houston RB **Joe Mixon** piled up 106 yards and a TD.

The Rams' Cobie Durant sacked Darnold.

Ravens 28, Steelers 14

The one-two punch of Ravens QB **Lamar Jackson** (2 TD passes) and RB **Derrick Henry** (186 yards and 2 TDs) was too much for the Steelers.

Bills 31, Broncos 7

Buffalo had little trouble with the up-and-coming Broncos. QB **Josh Allen** threw 2 TD passes, while the Bills D allowed only 224 total yards.

NFC

Eagles 22, Packers 10

Philly's D picked off **Jordan Love** three times and held the powerful Packers offense quiet. Philly TE **Dallas Goedert**'s 24-yard TD catch-and-run (complete with three stiff-arms of tacklers) was an Eagles highlight.

Commanders 23, Buccaneers 20

When **Zane Gonzalez** "doinked" in a 37-yard field goal, Washington won its first playoff game since 2005. (He bounced it off the upright!) A key fumble by Tampa Bay QB **Baker Mayfield** helped the Commanders come from behind to win.

Rams 27, Vikings 9

The game was moved to Arizona after terrible fires in Los Angeles. The Rams didn't care where they played. They sacked Vikings QB **Sam Darnold** nine times, intercepted him once, and forced a fumble that **Jared Verse** returned 57 yards for a TD.

Divisional Playoffs

AFC

Bills 27, Ravens 25

Turnovers doomed Baltimore in this game. Ravens QB **Lamar Jackson** threw an interception and fumbled once, while the Bills never turned the ball over. Buffalo QB **Josh Allen** rushed for 2 TDs. After a late TD, Ravens TE **Mark Andrews** dropped a pass on a two-point attempt that would have tied the score.

Chiefs 23, Texans 12

One QB stayed up and the other got knocked down . . . a lot. KC's **Patrick Mahomes** continued his hot play, including a miraculous TD pass to TE **Travis Kelce**. The KC defense sacked Houston's **C.J. Stroud** eight times.

Jayden Daniels

NFC

Commanders 45, Lions 31

In a huge upset, the Commanders forced 5 turnovers by the high-scoring Lions. The win sent Washington to its first NFC title game since 1991! The Commanders made 4 interceptions and recovered a fumble. Washington QB **Jayden Daniels** sure didn't look like a rookie, throwing for 299 yards with 2 TD passes.

Eagles 28, Rams 22

In a game played in cold and snow, Philly RB **Saquon Barkley** stayed hot, with TD runs of 78 and 62 yards to lead the Eagles. QB **Jalen Hurts** also had a 44-yard TD run. Two Rams fumbles sealed the deal for the Eagles.

AFC Championship

CHIEFS 32, BILLS 29

So close, but so far. For the fourth time, the Bills lost to the Chiefs in the playoffs. Buffalo came close this time but could not power through the big Chiefs defensive line when it counted most. Twice in the fourth quarter, Buffalo lost the ball on downs when it could not gain the single yard it needed to keep driving. Bills QB **Josh Allen** had scored 12 rushing TDs in 2024, but he could not power through on those two big plays. Those big stops were the difference between winning and losing. Buffalo also failed to score on a pair of two-point conversion attempts. Bills RB **James Cook** did have 2 rushing scores.

8 That's how many NFL teams have won back-to-back Super Bowls (and the Pittsburgh Steelers did it twice). However, through the 2024 season, no team had won three in a row. Would the Chiefs be the first?

The Chiefs, meanwhile, kept doing what they had done all year—play solid D and watch QB **Patrick Mahomes** work his magic. He scored 2 rushing TDs and passed for a third. He led the Chiefs to the last score, a game-winning 35-yard FG by **Harrison Butker** that broke up a tie game.

Allen got the first on this play, but the Chiefs stopped him later.

NFC Championship

EAGLES 55, COMMANDERS 24

The first time Eagles RB **Saquon Barkley** touched the football in this game, he ran for a 60-yard TD. The second time he touched it, he ran for a 4-yard TD. And he was just getting started! Philadelphia headed to its second Super Bowl in three seasons by running all over the Commanders. Barkley scored another TD in the fourth quarter and ended the day with 118 rushing yards. His QB, **Jalen Hurts**, was almost as good, smashing into the end zone three times himself. In all, the Eagles scored 7 rushing TDs.

Barkley leaped in for a key TD.

> ***"The goal wasn't just getting there. The goal is to win. We're going to celebrate and enjoy this . . . and get right back to work."***
>
> — EAGLES RB SAQUON BARKLEY

Jalen Hurts

The Philly D created 4 Commanders turnovers, including forcing 3 fumbles. Washington's rookie QB **Jayden Daniels** had a great season but hit the wall in this game, fumbling and throwing an interception. He did throw a TD pass and run for a score. At one point, the Commanders trailed by only 14-12. But the Eagles were just too much. They turned all 4 Commanders turnovers into touchdowns and ended Washington's dream season.

Philadelphia used this play—called the Brotherly Shove—to propel Hurts into the end zone.

SUPER BOWL LIX

Fly, Eagles, Fly!

Philadelphia Eagles 40, Kansas City Chiefs 22

That headline could also read, "Defend, Eagles, Defend!" The Eagles defense shut down star QB **Patrick Mahomes** and the Chiefs, leading the way to Philadelphia's big win. Mahomes had played 120 NFL games heading into the Super Bowl in New Orleans. But he had never been sacked six times, which Philly did in this game. They also picked off two of his passes, returning one for a TD. The second pick set up another Eagles TD. From almost the first play, the Eagles' defensive line was all over Mahomes. He never got the time to work his usual miracles.

The Eagles' offense was also excellent, marching steadily down the field. The Chiefs had planned to shut down Philly's all-world RB **Saquon Barkley**, and they mostly did. But QB **Jalen Hurts** stepped up and ran wild. He threw 2 TD passes and ran for another score, using his quick feet to make several big plays. Add in a perfect day for Eagles K **Jake Elliott**—4-for-4 on field goals—and it was total dominance.

The second time the Eagles got the ball, they drove 69 yards to the 1-yard line. Then the Eagles used the famous "Brotherly Shove" play, with two teammates helping

2,502

Barkley had only 57 rushing yards in this game, but that gave him this big new total. It was the most in NFL history for a full season, including playoffs.

Hurts was the MVP for his all-around success.

to push Hurts into the end zone. After an Eagles field goal, rookie **Cooper DeJean** scored a 38-yard pick-six for Philly—and on his birthday, which was a Super Bowl first!

After the Eagles pinned the Chiefs deep in their own end, LB **Zack Baun** dove to make a huge interception of a Mahomes throw. Two plays later, Hurts hit WR **A.J. Brown** with a 12-yard TD. That made the score 24-0 Eagles. That was tied for the second-biggest halftime lead in Super Bowl history! How good were the Eagles? In that first half, they scored 24 points . . . while allowing the Chiefs only 23 yards!

Smith caught a game-clinching TD.

The Eagles' D kept things rolling in the second half. After another Elliott FG, they forced the Chiefs to turn the ball over with a big fourth-down stop. **Avonte Maddox** leaped to knock down a pass that would have given the Chiefs a first down. On the very next play, Hurts threw a perfect 46-yard pass to WR **DeVonta Smith** for a TD, making it 34-0 and putting the game solidly out of reach.

The Chiefs finally scored with 34 seconds left in the third quarter. Mahomes threw to speedy rookie **Xavier Worthy**. The Chiefs added 2 more scores in the fourth quarter, but it was not nearly enough.

Philadelphia won its first Super Bowl since 2018 and its second ever. It also kept Mahomes and the Chiefs from becoming the first team to win three Super Bowls in a row. Hurts was named the MVP for his passing, running, and leadership.

2024 NFL Awards

MOST VALUABLE PLAYER
JOSH ALLEN
QB, BILLS

Saquon Barkley

OFFENSIVE PLAYER OF THE YEAR
SAQUON BARKLEY
RB, EAGLES

DEFENSIVE PLAYER OF THE YEAR
PATRICK SURTAIN II
CB, BRONCOS

OFFENSIVE ROOKIE OF THE YEAR
JAYDEN DANIELS
QB, COMMANDERS

DEFENSIVE ROOKIE OF THE YEAR
JARED VERSE
LB, RAMS

COMEBACK PLAYER OF THE YEAR
JOE BURROW
QB, BENGALS

COACH OF THE YEAR
KEVIN O'CONNELL
VIKINGS

NFL MAN OF THE YEAR
(COMMUNITY SERVICE)
ARIK ARMSTEAD
DE, JAGUARS

2024 NFL Leaders

43 TD PASSES
4,918 PASSING YARDS
Joe Burrow • Bengals

2,005 RUSHING YARDS
Saquon Barkley • Eagles

16 RUSHING TDS
James Cook • Bills
Jahmyr Gibbs • Lions
Derrick Henry • Ravens

127 RECEPTIONS
1,708 RECEIVING YARDS
17 RECEIVING TDS
Ja'Marr Chase • Bengals

17.5 SACKS
Trey Hendrickson • Bengals

173 TACKLES
Zaire Franklin • Colts

9 INTERCEPTIONS
Kerby Joseph • Lions

41 FIELD GOALS
Chris Boswell • Steelers

Joe Burrow

NFL FANTASY

Fantasy football players watched some new stars emerge in 2024. Here are the top scoring players from NFL.com's game. How did your team do?

POSITION/PLAYER/POINTS		
QB	**Lamar Jackson**	430.38
RB	**Jahmyr Gibbs**	362.90
WR	**Ja'Marr Chase**	403.00
TE	**Brock Bowers**	262.70
K	**Chris Boswell**	184.00
D/ST	**Broncos**	181.00

Bowers was a rookie fantasy star!

Flag Football Star

Flag football is one of the fastest-growing school and youth sports. Many high schools now have official girls' teams, and youth leagues can be found all over. The Maxwell Club in Philadelphia, which has been around since 1935, gives out awards to the best college and pro football players. In 2024, the club gave its first National Flag Football Player of the Year Award to **Ava Wallace** of the Texas Fury in Leander, Texas.

2025 Hall of Fame

Four players were elected to the Pro Football Hall of Fame for 2025. It's tied for the smallest class ever. Part of the reason it's tied is that there is a PFHOF rule that at least four players have to be added each year! Congrats to these all-time greats!

Eric Allen, DB

Allen was a ballhawk. That's football slang for a defensive player with a nose for interceptions. Allen had at least 1 pick in each of his 14 NFL seasons. He ended up with 54 for his career, 9 of which he took home for touchdowns. This six-time Pro Bowl selection played for the Eagles, Saints, and Raiders.

◀◀◀Jared Allen, DE

For 12 seasons, NFL QBs hated facing this pass-rushing machine. He had eight seasons with 11 or more sacks, leading the league in 2007 and 2011. His 22.0 sacks in 2011 (with the Vikings) are tied for second-most in a year. He was named first-team All-Pro four times. Great trivia: He is tied for the NFL all-time with 4 safeties! Allen played for the Chiefs, Vikings, Bears, and Panthers.

Antonio Gates, TE▶▶▶

In 16 seasons with the Chargers, Gates became one of the best ever at his tough position. A former college basketball star, he used his height and strength to haul in 955 catches. A whopping 116 of those went for touchdowns, the most ever among NFL tight ends. He is also the Chargers all-time leader in catches and receiving yards. Gates made eight Pro Bowls and had at least 7 TDs in each of 11 seasons.

Sterling Sharpe, WR

Sharpe played only seven seasons with the Packers, but he made the most of them. He led the NFL in catches three times, TD catches twice, and receiving yards once. He was a three-time first-team All-Pro. A neck injury cut his career short, but he has ended up in the Hall. His brother, TE **Shannon Sharpe**, is already a member. The Sharpes are the first brothers to be inducted into the PFHOF!

OHIO STATE
2025
1

COLLEGE FOOTBALL

A NEW NUMBER ONE
Ohio State RB Quinshon Judkins sprints away from Notre Dame defenders in the National Championship Game. Judkins and Ohio State were both No. 1 after his Buckeyes beat the Fighting Irish 34-23. OSU's big win capped off a great first season of the 12-team College Football Playoff. Read all the results and more right here!

College Football 2024

The 2024 college football season was all about change.

Players: In the old days, players could not move easily from school to school. But the "transfer portal," which sounds like something from a comic book movie, has changed that. Players are now allowed to transfer without having to sit out a year. Big-name quarterbacks were changing teams left and right. Heading into the 2024 season, five of the past six quarterbacks to win the Heisman Trophy were transfers. Plus, players can now make money. That changed only recently. They can be paid for the use of their name, image, and likeness (NIL). Some players made millions for their hard work and their contributions to the money that was flowing into their schools from TV and other sources.

Coaches: Coaching college football has always been hard. But now college football coaches have a new part of their job. They have to replace players who transferred, often by finding NIL money to pay them. Fewer players than ever are spending all their time at one school.

Schools: In the past few years, many top schools have changed the conferences they play in. In 2024, Texas and Oklahoma moved from the Big 12 to play in the SEC. BYU, Cincinnati, Central Florida, and Houston all joined the Big 12. USC and UCLA left the Pac-12 to join the Big Ten. As a result, the Pac-12 almost disappeared. Eight other teams left that conference in 2024, leaving only Oregon State and Washington State behind. How odd was this? California and Stanford, which are both less than 30 miles from the Pacific Ocean, moved to the *Atlantic* Coast Conference (ACC)!

Playoff: Finally, there was the new playoff plan. For the first time in 2024, the College Football Playoff, or CFP, would

Ashton Jeanty

feature 12 teams. The CFP had started in 2014, when only four teams made the field. Expanding to 12 was a huge move. But it was supported by most fans and players because it would give so many more teams a chance at winning the national championship.

Other than all of that, 2024 was just your average college football season! But could the excitement on the field during the 2024 season match what happened off the field before it started?

The answer is, of course, yes! Surprise teams, ranging from Colorado and Boise State to Indiana and SMU, captured hearts. Traditionally great teams, including Alabama, Michigan, Florida, and USC, broke others.

Wait a sec: UCLA and USC were in the Big Ten?

FINAL TOP 10

1. **Ohio State**
2. **Notre Dame**
3. **Oregon**
4. **Texas**
5. **Penn State**
6. **Georgia**
7. **Arizona State**
8. **Boise State**
9. **Tennessee**
10. **Indiana**

Teams continued to run up the scoreboard, with Miami leading the way at 43.9 points per game. A running back, Boise State's **Ashton Jeanty**, almost broke the all-time record for rushing yards in a season. There were last-second touchdowns and last-second field goals. There were winning plays that were overruled by replay, and there were plays that only became winning plays *after* being overruled by replay. And some things didn't change, such as debates about who should be ranked No. 1. A new Heisman Trophy winner, Colorado superstar **Travis Hunter**, thrilled everyone. And Army vs. Navy brought us all together in the end.

After the changes off the field, one of the greatest sports around delivered as it normally does. Major changes had led to major attention and lots of discussion. But, as always, the real excitement was on the field.

College football fans wouldn't have it any other way.

Hunter (left) showed off his defensive skills against Baylor by forcing this fumble.

August/September

Early Fall: The 2024 college football season started before the calendar hit September, and it started in far-off Dublin, Ireland. Georgia Tech upset No. 10 Florida State 24-21 on a field goal by **Aiden Birr** as time expired. Back in the USA, Montana State scored 2 TDs in the final five minutes to upset New Mexico State. Finally, SMU came from behind by outscoring Nevada 16-0 in the final quarter to beat the Wolf Pack, 29-24.

Welcome to the Big Ten: USC and LSU, which produced the last two Heisman winners (**Caleb Williams** and **Jayden Daniels**), started their seasons in Las Vegas. For USC, it was its first game as a member of the Big Ten Conference.

The Trojans hung in there until the end, then scored with only eight seconds left to win 27-20.

Welcome to the Big 12: Arizona visited Kansas State for its first conference game as a member of the Big 12. The host Wildcats treated the visiting Wildcats rudely, beating them 31-7.

Big Start in Boise: Boise State running back **Ashton Jeanty** started the season in style. He gained 267 yards in the Broncos' opening 56-45 win over Georgia Southern. He also scored a school-record 6 TDs! By the end of September, Jeanty had already rolled up 845 yards over the season's first four games. Now that was a Heisman-worthy start!

Double Trouble: Colorado fans stormed the field twice—in the same game! The first time they thought their Buffaloes had beaten Baylor in overtime. Two-way superstar **Travis Hunter** jarred the ball loose from Baylor's quarterback just before he went into the end zone: field storm No. 1. But officials had to review the play. So everyone off the field, please. Then, the referee confirmed the call: field storm No. 2! Oh, and the game went to overtime thanks to a Colorado Hail Mary! It's almost surprising the fans didn't storm the field *three* times! The Buffaloes won 38-31.

Replay It Forward: No. 7 Miami's fans thought their Hurricanes had stopped Virginia Tech's upset bid. They had seen a Miami defender emerge from an end zone pile with the ball on the last play of the game. But then the referees decided that Virginia Tech had come down with the Hail Mary pass and ruled the play a touchdown. But the replay booth disagreed, overturning the call! Final score: Miami 38, Virginia Tech 34.

Home Field Advantage: Alabama celebrated the 2024 season by naming its field after newly retired coach **Nick Saban**. But even Saban had never seen a wilder Alabama game than the one the No. 4 Crimson Tide played against rival No. 2 Georgia. The Tide took a surprising 30-7 lead into halftime before the Bulldogs pulled a shocker of their own, taking a 34-33 lead on a 67-yard pass with less than three minutes left. But one more shocker was still to come. Alabama scored on a 75-yard pass on the next play with just over two minutes left! Tide 41, Dawgs 34.

This TD catch by Ryan Williams turned the tide for Alabama.

October

Slim and None: No one gave Arkansas much of a chance against Tennessee. The Razorbacks were 3–2, but Tennessee was undefeated and ranked No. 4 in the country. Arkansas was the home team and trailed 14-10 entering the fourth quarter. But the Hogs scored nine unanswered points from there, winning the game on a touchdown with just over a minute left. Final score: Arkansas 19, Tennessee 14.

Not Slim, Just None: Later, no one gave Vanderbilt any chance against mighty Alabama. After all, Vanderbilt had never beaten a Top 5 team, and the Crimson Tide were ranked No. 1. And the Commodores had not beaten the Tide in 40 years. That all changed when Vandy QB **Diego Pavia** directed a 40-35 upset victory. No one was happier than the Vanderbilt fans, who tore down a goalpost and carried it for two miles outside the stadium before dumping it in the Cumberland River!

Too Much, Too Late: Almost nine months after Michigan beat Washington in the 2023 National Championship Game, the Huskies had their chance for revenge.

Pavia threw 2 TD passes to lead Vanderbilt to a huge upset over Alabama.

Georgia's Trevor Etienne battled Texas.

Not only that, but the team was playing the Wolverines in its home stadium in Seattle. Washington QB **Will Rogers** had 2 TD passes, and his Huskies won 27-17.

Too Little, Too Early: Little did anyone know in October, when Ohio State visited Oregon in what many would call the game of the year, that the two teams would play again in January's College Football Playoff. The Ducks held on in the teams' first matchup, as the clock hit zero soon after Buckeye QB **Will Howard** slid to try to stop it. Final score: Oregon 32, Ohio State 31.

Splash in Texas: When Georgia visited top-ranked Texas, they played one of the wildest games of the year. The Bulldogs built a big lead, but the Longhorns staged a second-half comeback. (Spoiler alert: Georgia and Texas would also play again later in the season, in the SEC Championship Game.) Then came a controversial pass-interference penalty against Texas. While the officials were reviewing the call, fans started throwing water bottles onto the field in protest! Looking at the replay, the officials changed their call. Georgia held on to win 30-15.

Syra-excuse Me: Fall weather was in full bloom when Syracuse visited Pitt in October. Unfortunately for Orange QB **Kyle McCord**, so were interceptions! The Ohio State transfer threw not 1 . . . not 2 . . . but *4* interceptions—3 of which were returned for touchdowns—in the first half alone! By the time the game was over, he had thrown 5 interceptions overall. Not surprisingly, Pitt won easily, 41-13.

We Love LA: On the same night as Game 1 of the Dodgers–Yankees World Series, USC beat Rutgers, which had traveled 3,000 miles to the game. USC won 42-20, but the loudest cheer of the night came when the Dodgers' **Freddie Freeman** hit a walk-off grand slam home run to beat the Yankees. Most of the fans were watching on their phones in between watching the Trojans play the Scarlet Knights.

Brandon George with one of Pitt's 5 picks

November/December

Elijah Sarratt rambled for an Indiana touchdown.

A November to Remember: That's an old saying in college football, and it's true. For November—and now December as well—is when championship seasons are made. Unfortunately for Army, which entered its annual game against Notre Dame unbeaten at 9–0, the mighty Irish were too much for the Black Knights. Notre Dame jumped out to a 28-7 lead at halftime, eventually winning the game 49-14.

Not Bad for a Basketball School: Indiana the state and Indiana the university have a long and famous basketball history. In 2024, the school added some football success. The Hoosiers were 10–1 entering their regular-season finale against archrival Purdue. Purdue is also a basketball school, and it certainly played like one. By the time the game was over, Indiana had won 66-0.

Upset Stomach: There is nothing more fun in college football than a big upset. How about when three major upsets happen on the same day? The first weekend in November kicked off with three losses by unbeaten teams—Penn State, Iowa State, and Pittsburgh. The three winners in those games? Ohio State, Texas Tech, and SMU.

Buckeyes Bounced: The year 2024 was when Ohio State was supposed to finally stop its losing streak against archrival Michigan. The Buckeyes were No. 2 going into the game, while Michigan limped into the OSU stadium with a 6–5 record. But "that's why they play the games." Not only did the Wolverines pull off the 13-10 upset, but the Buckeyes lost their cool afterward, resulting in an ugly fight on the field.

Not Bad for a Rookie: This season marked Arizona State's first year in the Big 12. And it wasted no time making itself feel at home in its new conference. The Sun Devils had been picked last in the conference in preseason polls. But there they stood at the end of the Big 12 Championship Game, having defeated Iowa State 45-19. Pretty good for the new kid on the block.

From the Big 12 to the SEC: Texas A&M left the Big 12 for the SEC in 2012.

Twelve years later, Texas did the same. By the end of the 2024 season, the longtime rivals found themselves playing each other for the right to play Georgia in the SEC Championship Game. No one was happier about this surprising turn of events than Longhorn fans, who cheered their team to a 17-7 victory.

A Military Battle: Army and Navy have been playing each other in football since 1890. In 2024, the Black Knights and the Midshipmen met with a combined record of 19–4. Army, at 11–1, was favored over 8–3 Navy and had already won the American Athletic Conference championship. So, how about another upset? Final score: Navy 31, Army, 13. Go Navy, Beat Army!

Michigan QB Alex Orji led an upset.

Brandon Chatman of Navy used the ground game to score against Army.

Conference Championships

This TD by Georgia's Etienne gave the Bulldogs an exciting overtime win.

Winning a conference championship was more important than ever in 2024 (see page 70). The first five shown here earned automatic spots in the CFP. Other Playoff spots were on the line in many of these games, along with the joy of being a champion.

THE BIG FIVE

ATLANTIC COAST CONFERENCE

Clemson 34, SMU 31

A back-and-forth game came down to the final play. Clemson had snuck into the game after Miami was upset in the final regular-season game. The Tigers stormed out to a 24-7 halftime lead, but SMU QB **Kevin Jennings** threw 3 TD passes in the second half to help SMU tie the game at 31-31. There were only 16 seconds left, but Clemson's **Adam Randall** returned a kickoff for 41 yards. One play later, **Nolan Hauser** hit a 56-yard field goal to win the game.

BIG TEN

Oregon 45
Penn State 37

In its first season in the Big Ten, Oregon remained unbeaten in 2024 with a high-scoring win. QB **Dillon Gabriel** led the way with 4 TD passes. **Jordan James** and **Kenyon Sadiq** each scored 2 TDs for the Ducks. Penn State made it close, coming within eight points in the fourth quarter, but Gabriel directed a long drive that ended with James' final TD. A late score by Penn State was not enough.

BIG 12 Arizona State 45 Iowa State 19

This was ASU's first season in the Big 12 (which actually has 16 teams). They had been picked to finish last by preseason experts. Those experts were wrong. The Sun Devils rolled over the Cyclones to win the conference title and earn a bye in the Playoff bracket. RB **Cam Skattebo** was the ground-pounding star, running for 170 yards and 2 TDs. He caught a pass for another score. QB **Sam Leavitt** had 3 TD passes.

MOUNTAIN WEST Boise State 29 UNLV 24

Boise State earned a surprise bye with its conference title win. They were led by Heisman Trophy runner-up RB **Ashton Jeanty**, who had 128 rushing yards and a TD. University of Nevada, Las Vegas came back from being behind at halftime to take the lead in the third quarter. But the Broncos marched 75 yards to Jeanty's TD for the game's final score.

SEC Georgia 22 Texas 19 (OT)

Both teams figured to make the CFP, but only one would earn the important bye. Georgia was down to its third-string QB, **Gunner Stockton**, after injuries to other players. But he led his team to the lead late in the game. Texas rallied and tied it at 16-16 before regular time ended. In overtime, the Longhorns got a field goal. Then Stockton moved his team to near the goal line. A hard hit knocked him out, so injured starter **Carson Beck** handed off to RB **Trevor Etienne**, who scored the game-winner.

OTHER CONFERENCES

AAC Army 35, Tulane 14

The Black Knights won their first AAC championship behind the power running of **Bryson Daily**. He scored 4 TDs. Army RB **Kanye Udoh** helped with 158 rushing yards. The win sent Army into the CFP.

MAC Ohio 38, Miami (OH) 3

Ohio University (not Ohio State!) won the MAC title for the first time since 1968. QB **Parker Navarro** was a powerhouse, throwing 2 TD passes and rushing for a pair of scores as well.

SWAC Jackson State 41, Southern 13

QB **Zy McDonald** made sure that Jackson State kept up its great run, leading them to their third title in four seasons. McDonald threw a TD pass and also ran for 95 yards and a TD.

SUN BELT Marshall 31, Louisiana 3

The Thundering Herd set a record for biggest winning margin in conference title-game history. QB **Braylon Braxton** led the way, throwing 2 TD passes and adding a pair of rushing TDs.

Zy McDonald

College Football Playoff

In 2024, the College Football Playoff expanded from 4 to 12 teams. Teams were still ranked all season, but the final 12 were chosen by a special committee. They had to pick the five highest-ranked conference champions. The top four of those five earned a bye, which meant they moved right to the second round. Seven more teams were chosen to fill out the bracket. Those seven and the remaining conference champ played in the first round, leaving eight teams for the second round. The winners moved to the semifinals, and then those winners to the championship game. Whew! It was a lot of football, and fans loved every minute!

Blue (left) and Texas romped over Clemson.

Notre Dame 27, Indiana 17

The 2024 College Football Playoff kicked off in famous Notre Dame Stadium! The atmosphere was electric as Indiana and Notre Dame took the field. The electricity continued for the Irish, who scored on their third play of the game on a 98-yard run by **Jeremiyah Love**. The Irish never trailed, taking a 27-3 lead before the Hoosiers scored 2 late touchdowns.

Penn State 38, SMU 10

SMU was the last team to make the College Football Playoff. Could the upstart Mustangs compete with the mighty Penn State Nittany Lions? Not on this freezing day in State College, Pennsylvania. SMU QB **Kevin Jennings** threw 3 interceptions, 2 of which were returned for touchdowns as Penn State took a 28-0 halftime lead. The Mustangs never got back into the game in the second half.

Texas 38, Clemson 24

There was a lot of orange on the field when Texas took on Clemson in the CFP. The Longhorns took a commanding 28-10 lead at halftime. But the Tigers mounted a comeback, closing to within 31-24 in the fourth quarter. Texas' rushing attack was too much in the end, as RBs **Jaydon Blue** and **Quintrevion Wisner** each ran for more than 100 yards.

Star WR Smith scores for Ohio State.

Ohio State 42, Tennessee 17

Tennessee at Ohio State was the last of the first-round playoff games. Would fans finally be able to enjoy a close game? Ohio State made sure they would not. The Buckeyes scored touchdowns on their first three drives, enabling them to jump out to a 21-0 lead. One TD came from star freshman WR **Jeremiah Smith**. They repeated the feat in the second half, scoring on their first three drives to put the Volunteers away.

CFP Quarterfinals

Drew Allar

Fiesta Bowl Penn State 31 Boise State 14

Could Penn State's awesome defense stop Heisman runner-up **Ashton Jeanty**? This was the main question going into the Fiesta Bowl. The answer was . . . yes. While Jeanty rushed for 104 yards, he averaged only 3.5 yards per carry, just half of his season average. In the meantime, Nittany Lions QB **Drew Allar** heated up at the right time, throwing 3 touchdown passes.

Peach Bowl Texas 39 Arizona State 31 (2OT)

Finally, a close game! No one gave Arizona State much of a chance to upset mighty Texas. But the Sun Devils made things hard on the Longhorns in the most exciting playoff game to date. Texas took a 24-8 lead in the fourth quarter. That's when Arizona State RB **Cam Skattebo** took over, leading a wild comeback that forced overtime. In OT, the Longhorns had to make a fourth-down TD to continue. In the end, Texas survived, winning the game in the second OT.

Rose Bowl Ohio State 41 Oregon 21

Oregon entered the Rose Bowl as the nation's only unbeaten team. And the Ducks had already beaten Ohio State in the regular season. Advantage Oregon, right? Then they kicked off, and the Buckeyes took over from there. By the time the Ducks realized what was happening, they were down 34-0—and it wasn't even halftime yet! Ohio State had 4 TDs of 40 or more yards.

Sugar Bowl Notre Dame 23 Georgia 10

Georgia walked into the Sugar Bowl having won the powerful Southeastern Conference, not to mention two of the last three national championships. The Bulldogs outgained Notre Dame in the game. The only problem is that they forgot to protect the ball. Georgia lost 2 fumbles, including one inside its own 20-yard line.

Ohio State coach Ryan Day (with beard) watches LB Sawyer race to the clinching TD.

CFP Semifinals

Orange Bowl **Notre Dame 27** **Penn State 24**

The stakes were high for Notre Dame and Penn State, with the Orange Bowl winner moving on to the National Championship Game. And both teams played like they wanted to be there. The Nittany Lions had the ball with less than a minute left. The game was tied. But the Irish intercepted a pass. With seven seconds remaining, Notre Dame's **Mitch Jeter** kicked a field goal to win the game. An instant classic was complete.

Cotton Bowl **Ohio State 28** **Texas 14**

Perhaps the most dramatic play in the 2024 Playoff was the one Ohio State DE **Jack Sawyer** made with two minutes left in the Cotton Bowl. Texas had the ball on the Ohio State 8-yard line with a chance to tie the game. But Sawyer knocked the ball out of Longhorn QB **Quinn Ewers**' hands and scooped it up. As his teammates and fans went wild, he rambled 83 yards for the clinching touchdown. By the time he reached the end zone, he was a Buckeye legend!

National Championship Game

OHIO STATE 34, NOTRE DAME 23

Judkins stretched out for a big OSU TD.

And so it all came down to this.

Two of history's most famous college football programs—Notre Dame and Ohio State—met for the national championship. The Irish and the Buckeyes came into the game with 19 national titles between them: 11 for Notre Dame, 8 for Ohio State. Who would add to their collection and win the 2024 College Football Playoff?

At first it seemed like the answer would be Notre Dame. The Irish took charge early, marching 75 yards for a touchdown on the game's first possession. Not only that, but they took nearly 10 minutes to do it! The Buckeyes had a powerful offense, but if Notre Dame could dominate time of possession, OSU would be in trouble.

But then Ohio State got the ball. And they scored. And they scored again. And then they scored again. By the time the Notre Dame defense—not to mention the Irish fans—could realize what was happening, the Buckeyes had reeled off 31 straight points! Three TDs came on runs or catches by RB **Quinshon Judkins**. Halfway through the third quarter, it looked like the rout was on.

But wait! Notre Dame didn't make it this far without being a great team. And

Notre Dame QB Leonard

great teams never quit. The Irish scored 2 late touchdowns to cut the lead to eight with less than five minutes left. Both TDs came on passes from **Riley Leonard** to WR **Jaden Greathouse**. Notre Dame also made a pair of two-point conversions. If the Irish could keep Ohio State from scoring, they would have one last chance to tie the game and send it to overtime.

But that's the other thing about great teams—they always respond. The Buckeyes closed things out. The game came down to a third-and-11 for Ohio State on its own 34-yard line. QB **Will Howard** stepped back, planted his foot and threw the ball as far as he could. Fifty-seven yards later, it fell right into the arms of WR **Jeremiah Smith**! Ohio State had a first down with the ball inside Notre Dame's 10-yard line with time running out. When **Jayden Fielding**'s field goal gave the Buckeyes an 11-point lead, the Irish were out of their famous luck. The victory gave OSU its first national title since 2014.

Smith's late catch helped the Buckeyes clinch the national title.

"And there was a point at the end of the year where there's nobody who thought we were going to do this . . . I think there's a lot of life lessons to be learned [from that]."

—OSU COACH RYAN DAY

2024 CFB Awards

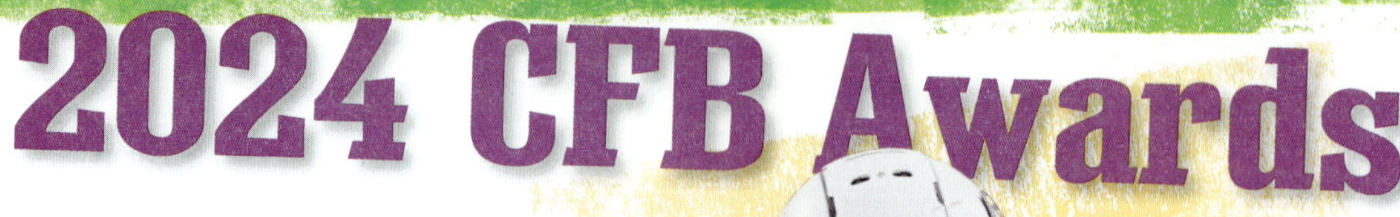

HEISMAN TROPHY (OVERALL)
WALTER CAMP AWARD (OVERALL)
BILETNIKOFF AWARD (WR)
BEDNARIK AWARD (DEFENSE)

Travis Hunter, Colorado

BRONKO NAGURSKI TROPHY (DEFENSE)

Kyle Kennard
South Carolina

BUTKUS AWARD (LB)

Jalon Walker, Georgia

DAVEY O'BRIEN AWARD (QB)

Cam Ward, Miami

DOAK WALKER AWARD (RB)
MAXWELL AWARD (OVERALL)

Ashton Jeanty
Boise State

JIM THORPE AWARD (DB)

Jahdae Barron, Texas

OUTLAND TROPHY (LINEMAN)

Kelvin Banks Jr.
Texas

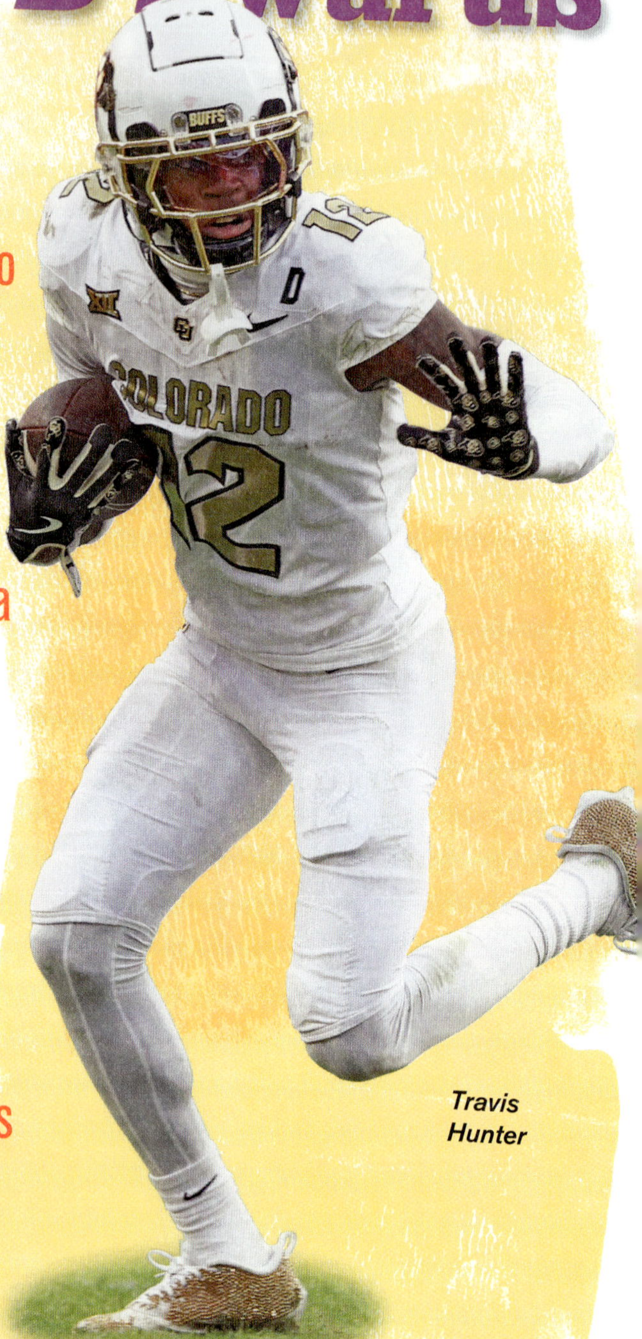

Travis Hunter

Other NCAA Champs

The College Football Playoff gets all the attention, but there are hundreds of other schools aiming for a national title. The NCAA has four other divisions, each of which plays a championship tournament. Here are the winners for the 2024 season.

FCS Division

North Dakota State 35
Montana State 32

The Bison of NDSU are a lower-division dynasty. This was their tenth national title and first since 2021. This game came down to a wild fourth quarter. NDSU led 21-18, but then both teams scored 2 touchdowns in the final 15 minutes. The last got Montana State within three points, but they couldn't find another score. NDSU QB **Cam Miller** was awesome, throwing for 2 TDs and rushing for 121 yards and 2 more scores.

Miller races for a big TD.

Division II

Ferris State (Michigan) 49
Valdosta State (Georgia) 14

Ferris State continued a great run, winning its third championship in four seasons. They scored 2 TDs in each of the first three quarters and ran away with the game.

Division III

North Central (Illinois) 41
UW–Whitewater (Wisconsin) 14

Talk about a powerhouse! North Central won its third title in four seasons and won every game in 2024 by more than 16 points! QB **Luke Lehnen** led the way after winning his second-straight Gagliardi Trophy as the top D-III player.

NAIA

Grand View (Iowa) 35
Keiser (Florida) 7

Both teams began the game undefeated, but only Grand View ended that way. QB **Jackson Waring** had 4 TD passes for Grand View, 2 of them to WR **Aisea Toki**.

WNBA/NBA

GIVE US LIBERTY!
Breanna Stewart and the New York Liberty won their first WNBA championship in 2025, beating the Minnesota Lynx in a thrilling five-game series. It was the end of a breakout season for the WNBA, which reached new highs in popularity and viewers. Get the whole story inside!

A NEW CHAMP!
Jalen Williams and the Oklahoma City Thunder won their first NBA title, beating the Indiana Pacers in an exciting seven-game series. The Thunder used to be the Seattle SuperSonics and won it all in 1979. But this was the first in their new home. *Check out the whole season on page 92!*

WNBA: What a Year!

A'ja Wilson

The 2024 WNBA season was its biggest and best yet. New stars were attracting millions of fans. Superstars were piling up all-time records. TV ratings rose, and the league set attendance records left and right. In its 28th season, the WNBA hit the big time.

We'll get to famous rookies in a moment, but first, huge props to **A'ja Wilson** for what some experts called the best season in league history. She was a unanimous MVP (the first since 1997!) after setting all-time single-season records with 1,021 total points and a 26.9 points-per-game average. Showing that she is the total player, she also led the league with 451 rebounds (another single-season WNBA record) and 98 blocks. No one had ever led all three categories in the same season! Wilson also moved into first place all-time with a 21.07 points-per-game average.

While Wilson was setting records, she was joined in the spotlight by two rookies—**Caitlin Clark** and **Angel Reese**. Clark broke college scoring records at Iowa and joined the Indiana Fever as the top overall draft pick. She then broke just about every WNBA rookie record and led the Indiana Fever back to the playoffs. Fellow first-year star Reese of the Chicago Sky dominated at both ends of the court and set a new league record with 15 straight double-doubles (a game with double digits in two stat categories). There's lots more on this awesome pair on pages 84–85!

The WNBA took a break to let its players dominate at the Summer Olympics. In all, 51 current or former WNBA stars played for

11 countries at the Games in Paris. The US team–with all 12 members from the WNBA–won gold for the eighth straight time. Six WNBA players were part of the Australian bronze-medal team, too.

Back on the court at home, the fast start by the Connecticut Sun was an early-season top story. Led by **Alyssa Thomas** and **Brionna Jones**, the Sun didn't lose until their tenth game. The New York Liberty were hot on their heels, opening up 12–2 behind the scoring punch of 2023 MVP **Breanna Stewart**. By midseason, the Liberty were well ahead, with a 15–3 record. The two-time defending champion Las Vegas Aces struggled, though. They were 6–6 at one point but ended up fourth in the regular season.

Thomas led the Sun to the playoffs.

2024 WNBA STANDINGS

1. **New York Liberty**	32–8
2. **Minnesota Lynx**	30–10
3. **Connecticut Sun**	28–12
4. **Las Vegas Aces**	27–13
5. **Seattle Storm**	25–15
6. **Indiana Fever**	20–20
7. **Phoenix Mercury**	19–21
8. **Atlanta Dream**	15–25
9. **Washington Mystics**	14–26
10. **Chicago Sky**	13–27
11. **Dallas Wings**	9–31
12. **Los Angeles Sparks**	8–32

A surprise team was the Minnesota Lynx, picked by most experts to miss the playoffs. The Lynx are four-time WNBA champs, but their last title came in 2017. In 2024, they stormed through the second half of the season, winning 13 of 15 games (and the Commissioner's Cup earlier). Would they return to the top of the league?

The regular season ended with a new single-game attendance record. A total of 20,771 fans watched the Washington Mystics beat Clark's Fever. It was a fitting end to a season that saw more fans than ever watch and enjoy WNBA games.

WNBA Notes

More on the Way!

In 2025, the WNBA will add a team in the San Francisco Bay Area: the Golden State Valkyries (the team name is from Norse mythology). The league also announced a new team will start in Toronto in 2026. A third new club, based in Portland, Oregon, will also start in 2026. The WNBA is big . . . and getting bigger! In 2025, the teams will play the longest season in league history, at 44 games. Also in 2025, the WNBA Finals will expand to best of seven from best of five.

A Great Night

One of the highlight plays of the year came in an August game. The Chicago Sky trailed the Aces by as many as 13 points in the fourth quarter. But they stormed back to tie the game on **Chennedy Carter**'s three-point shot. With just 1.2 seconds left, **Chelsea Gray** of the Aces lobbed an inbounds pass to **A'ja Wilson**, who sank the layup as time ran out, giving Vegas a 77-75 win. There must have been something in the air in the WNBA. On that very same night, the Dallas Wings tied a WNBA record by coming back from 19 points down in the fourth quarter to beat the Los Angeles Sparks 113-110.

Chelsea Gray

Ogunbowale (left) dominated the All-Star Game.

All-Star Game Upset

The US Olympic basketball team is like the all-star of All-Star teams. So what happened when the best of the WNBA played the best of the WNBA who hadn't made the Olympics? The players who would watch the Games on TV won! Led by 34 points (all in the second half!) from **Arike Ogunbowale**, the WNBA All-Stars shocked Team USA 117-109 in the 2024 WNBA All-Star Game. **Breanna Stewart** had a 31 points/10 rebounds double-double for Team USA (an all-time All-Star Game first), but it wasn't enough. Ogunbowale won her second All-Star Game MVP award.

Rebound GOAT

On the season's final day, **Tina Charles** of the Atlanta Dream became the WNBA's all-time top rebounder. Her career total reached 4,014 boards. That topped former No. 1 **Sylvia Fowles**. Charles also reached 194 double-doubles for her career, another new all-time record. To make the night even more special, she led the Dream to a win that clinched a playoff spot!

GOODBYE TO NO.1

Diana Taurasi is one of the most successful athletes of the 2000s and maybe the best woman's hoopster ever. The high-scoring guard won a record six Olympic gold medals (including 2024), three WNBA titles with Phoenix, and was named to 11 All-Star teams. Her 10,646 points and 1,447 three-pointers are the most in WNBA history. Teammates and opponents marveled at her fierce, all-around game. Taurasi retired in February 2025, wrapping up 20 years of world basketball success.

A lot was expected of Clark (left) . . . and she delivered big-time!

Rookie Wonders

Caitlin Clark

In college at Iowa, Clark had broken all the college scoring records and then was the first pick of the WNBA Draft. She came into the league with huge hype and lots of pressure. She soon found that things in the pros were a bit tougher than in college. The Indiana Fever lost its first five games and 10 of its first 13. Early on, Clark struggled, setting a first-game record with 10 turnovers. But she slowly got the hang of the pro game . . . and then some! By the time the regular season wrapped up, she had set these all-time WNBA records:

- Single-season record 337 assists
- Single-game record 19 assists
- Second-most three-pointers in a season (122)
- First rookie with a triple-double in a game

CAITLIN CLARK Rookie Records

These are some of Clark's all-time WNBA single-season rookie records set in 2024:

769 POINTS

19.2 POINTS PER GAME AVERAGE

122 THREE-POINTERS

337 ASSISTS

MOST **20**-POINT, **10**-ASSIST GAMES

- Fastest player to reach 500 points and 200 assists
- First rookie season with more than 500 points, 250 assists, and 75 three-pointers

Not surprisingly, Clark was the overwhelming choice as Rookie of the Year. She also made the All-WNBA First Team and All-Rookie First Team. Most important for Fever fans, she led the team back to the playoffs for the first time since 2016!

Angel Reese

While Clark was pouring in points, Reese was ripping down boards. She led the WNBA by averaging 13.1 rebounds per game. Her total of 446 rebounds was second-most in the league for 2024. At one point, she held a WNBA single-season record for rebounds before MVP **A'ja Wilson** later topped Reese to finish with a new record at 451. Reese also had a first-ever streak of three games with at least 20 rebounds.

Reese did not just rebound—she also scored in bunches. She had 15 double-doubles in a row (a new WNBA record), among her 26 total in that category. If not for a wrist injury late in the season, she would have surely added to all those totals. Few rookies have been as dominant under the glass as Reese.

Angel Reese

WNBA Playoffs

First Round

New York 2, Atlanta 0

Sabrina Ionescu poured in 36 points to lead the Liberty to a comeback win in Game 2.

Connecticut 2, Indiana 0

Caitlin Clark's great rookie season ended with a sweep by the Sun.

Minnesota 2, Phoenix 0

In the Lynx's two wins, the team scored a total of 203 points. **Napheesa Collier** had 80 of them, dominating play at both ends of the court. She scored 42 points in Game 2, tying a WNBA single-game playoff record. The series also marked the end of Phoenix star **Diana Taurasi**'s 20-year career (see page 83).

High scoring by Ionescu (right) led the Liberty to a first-round win.

Collier (right) had a dominant semifinal series for Minnesota.

Las Vegas 2, Seattle 0

A double-double from MVP **A'ja Wilson** (24 points, 13 rebounds) led the way to a Las Vegas sweep. The Aces returned to the semifinals for the sixth season in a row.

Semifinals

New York 3, Las Vegas 1

In a rematch of the 2023 WNBA Finals, the Liberty struck first. New York megastar **Breanna Stewart** poured in 34 points, while teammate Ionescu added 21. The Liberty won Game 1 87-77. New York then won Game 2 88-84, led by Ionescu's 24 points. After Vegas won Game 3 95-81, the Liberty earned their sixth trip to the WNBA Finals with a 76-62 Game 4 win, revenge for Vegas beating New York in the 2023 Finals.

Minnesota 3, Connecticut 2

The Sun won Game 1 on the road, beating the Lynx 73-70. They had to wait for a last-shot three-pointer to miss, however, showing how closely the two teams were matched. The Lynx tied the series with a 77-70 win. They took a series lead in Game 3 with a 90-81 win, led by Collier's 26-point double-double. But the Sun rallied to win Game 4 92-82 with a great defensive effort, forcing 13 turnovers. In Game 5, the Lynx led by as many as 21 points before cruising to an 88-77 win. Collier became the first player ever with three straight playoff games with at least 25 points and 10 rebounds.

EPIC WNBA Finals!

It was only right that the WNBA's best season ended with one of its all-time best series. Both the Liberty and Lynx battled to the final buzzer of each game, with superstars and role players stepping up to make big shots. It was a great end to a great season!

GAME 1 Lynx 95, Liberty 93

What a way to start the Finals! This game was an instant classic. Led by **Breanna Stewart** and **Sabrina Ionescu**, the Liberty stormed out to a big lead in front of their home fans. At one point, they were up by 18 points. But the Lynx never quit, even when down by 15 points with less than five minutes left. They slowly chipped away at the lead, getting closer and closer. Lynx guard **Courtney Williams** knocked down a three-point shot with 5.1 seconds left. She was fouled, making it a four-point play that put Minnesota up by one. Stewart then

What a shot! Ionescu's long three-point bucket clinched a huge Game 3 win for New York.

tied the game with a free throw and could have won it with another . . . but missed! In overtime, the Lynx led most of the way. The Liberty tied the game with less than a minute to go, but the Lynx won 95-93 on **Napheesa Collier**'s late basket! What a game!

GAME 2 Liberty 80, Lynx 66

The Lynx tried to come back like they did in Game 1, but they could not do it again. Stewart poured in 21 points to lead the Liberty to a series-tying win in front of the Liberty home fans. New York's 12-0 run to end the game sealed the deal.

GAME 3 Liberty 80, Lynx 77

Just like the Lynx did in Game 1, the Liberty came back from behind to get a clutch win. Minnesota led by as many as 15 points in the first half, but New York didn't quit. They tied the game in the fourth quarter. Then, with about 90 seconds to go, they took their first lead since early in the game. The Lynx tied it up again at 77-77. With just one second left, Ionescu calmly buried a long three-point shot to clinch the victory. Her shot from well outside the three-point line was one of the sports highlights of the year!

GAME 4 Lynx 82, Liberty 80

Another classic game gave WNBA fans all they wanted. The teams combined for a total of 27 ties or lead changes. Stewart started out cold but heated up. The teams kept it tight right to the end. With less than 20 seconds left, it was tied 80-80. Going for a winning shot, Williams missed for Minnesota. Trying to put in the rebound, **Bridget Carleton** of the Lynx was fouled. She made both free throws with two seconds left for the winning points. The teams headed to Game 5!

Stewart with the WNBA trophy

GAME 5 Liberty 67, Lynx 62

No one wanted the season to end, but it had to. The Liberty needed overtime, but they won their first WNBA championship. New York was one of the league's original teams and had even taken part in the first-ever game in 1997. They had reached the Finals five times but never came home a winner. Finally, in 2024, they did it! For most of Game 5, superstars Stewart and Ionescu struggled, missing most of their shots. The Lynx were up by 12 points in the first half at one point. But New York kept grinding, led by another former WNBA MVP, **Jonquel Jones**. She powered in 17 points, while her defense slowed the Lynx attack. Still, Stewart had to hit two key free throws with 5.2 seconds left in regulation to tie the game 60-60 and force OT. In the extra period, the Lynx went cold. They missed all their shots and could only score two free throws. A late steal clinched the game for New York! Jones was named the WNBA Finals MVP.

2024 WNBA Awards

MOST VALUABLE PLAYER

A'JA WILSON • ACES

DEFENSIVE PLAYER OF THE YEAR

NAPHEESA COLLIER
LYNX

ROOKIE OF THE YEAR

CAITLIN CLARK • FEVER

SIXTH PLAYER OF THE YEAR

TIFFANY HAYES • ACES

COMEBACK PLAYER OF THE YEAR

SKYLAR DIGGINS-SMITH • STORM

MOST IMPROVED PLAYER

DIJONAI CARRINGTON
SUN

COACH OF THE YEAR

CHERYL REEVE • LYNX

ALL-WNBA FIRST TEAM

A'JA WILSON*
NAPHEESA COLLIER*
BREANNA STEWART
ALYSSA THOMAS
CAITLIN CLARK

*Unanimous selection

Caitlin Clark

2024 WNBA Stat Leaders

(per-game averages, except for three-pointer total)

26.9 POINTS
2.6 BLOCKS
A'Ja Wilson • ACES

13.1 REBOUNDS
Angel Reese
SKY

8.4 ASSISTS
Caitlin Clark
FEVER

122 THREE-POINTERS
Caitlin Clark
FEVER

2.1 STEALS
Arike Ogunbowale
WINGS

Angel Reese

NBA 2024–25

Basketball is a team game. All five players on a team have to contribute, and all the bench players have roles, too. The superstars get all the attention, but experts know that a complete team wins championships. That was true in 2024 when the Boston Celtics proved to be much more than just **Jayson Tatum** and **Jaylen Brown**. In the 2024–25 season, balanced teams like the Oklahoma City Thunder, Cleveland Cavaliers, Indiana Pacers, and Houston Rockets showed that sharing the load was the way to the top.

The Thunder dominated the Western Conference, winning by 16 games. Yes, they did have the league MVP in **Shai Gilgeous-Alexander** (known as "SGA"). But he had a full cast of helpers at every position, and this proved a winning combo. In fact, the Thunder had an average winning margin of 12.9 points per game, the most ever in an NBA regular season. In the East, the Cavs were led by six-time All-Star **Donovan Mitchell**. Cleveland got out to a record hot start. They were the first team ever to win its first 10 games and score at least 110 points in each. They went 15–0 before their first loss! They ended up with the most wins in the Eastern Conference.

Meanwhile, the biggest news of the regular season came in February when the Dallas Mavericks traded superstar **Luka Dončić** to the Los Angeles Lakers. He joined **LeBron James** there to form one of the most powerful one-two punches in the league. The trade shocked Mavs fans, who loved their 25-year-old five-time All-Star. Dončić was surprised, too! The Lakers gave up another star, **Anthony Davis**, in the trade. Did it work out? Well, the Lakers made the playoffs with the West's third-best record but lost in the first round to the more well-rounded Minnesota Timberwolves.

Luka Dončić

In another big trade, **Jimmy Butler** joined the Golden State Warriors, giving the great **Stephen Curry** a proven winner to help him. It paid off with a strong playoff run from the seventh seed.

Having a stack of superstars did not prove to be a sure bet in 2024–25. The

Detroit's Cade Cunningham

Philadelphia 76ers added the great **Paul George** to a team that already included **Joel Embiid** and **Tyrese Maxey**. But injuries kept the top trio apart for much of the season, and Philly missed the playoffs. The Phoenix Suns paid their players more than any other team. They featured megastars **Kevin Durant**, **Devin Booker**, and **Bradley Beal**. It didn't work out, and the Suns finished under .500.

In 2023–24, the Detroit Pistons had one of the worst seasons in NBA history, losing 68 games while winning only 14. But they rallied and in 2024–25 had a huge turnaround. They won 44 games and made the playoffs for the first time since 2019.

With the top teams locked in by March as the season headed to the finish line, there were a lot of playoff spots still up for grabs. On the season's final weekend, the Western Conference still had to sort out seeds 4 through 10!

The playoffs included even more excitement and some surprises. See who rose to the top of the NBA in the pages ahead!

2024–25 REGULAR SEASON STANDINGS

EASTERN CONFERENCE

ATLANTIC DIVISION		CENTRAL DIVISION		SOUTHEAST DIVISION	
Celtics	61–21	Cavaliers	64–18	Magic	41–41
Knicks	51–31	Pacers	50–32	Hawks	40–42
Raptors	30–52	Bucks	48–34	Heat	37–45
Nets	26–56	Pistons	44–38	Hornets	19–63
76ers	24–58	Bulls	39–43	Wizards	18–64

WESTERN CONFERENCE

NORTHWEST DIVISION		SOUTHWEST DIVISION		PACIFIC DIVISION	
Thunder	68–14	Rockets	52–30	Lakers	50–32
Nuggets	50–32	Grizzlies	48–34	Clippers	50–32
Timberwolves	49–33	Mavericks	39–43	Warriors	48–34
Trail Blazers	36–46	Spurs	34–48	Kings	40–42
Jazz	17–65	Pelicans	21–61	Suns	36–46

In the Paint

An NBA first: Bronny and LeBron played together!

Hi, Dad!: The NBA season tipped off with history. In the Lakers' 110-103 win over the Timberwolves, **LeBron James** and his son **Bronny** became the first father-son pair to appear in the same NBA game. Bronny was a rookie from USC, while of course James is "the King," the NBA's all-time leading scorer.

50-Point News: Paolo Banchero of the Magic was the first player to hit 50 points in a game. He had exactly that many in Orlando's 119-115 win over Indiana. It was his first time reaching the half-century mark. Later, **Shai Gilgeous-Alexander** of the Thunder had four 50-point games in less than two months; he was the 12th player ever with a quartet of 50s in a season.

Can't Win 'em All: In December, the Golden State Warriors lost to the Memphis Grizzlies 144-93. The 51-point margin was the biggest of the season. For the first time in his career (in a game that he played at least 12 minutes), **Stephen Curry** didn't score a single field goal. Ouch.

NBA Cup: The Milwaukee Bucks had a pretty good season, winning 48 games and making the playoffs. But even though they lost in the first round to Indiana, they did get some hardware. In December, the Bucks beat the Thunder to win the NBA Cup, the league's in-season tournament. **Giannis Antetokounmpo** had a triple-double (including a game-high 26 points) in the 97-81 win in Las Vegas.

Amazing Finish: The Chicago Bulls trailed the Lakers by a point with just seconds left. Chicago's **Josh Giddey** got the ball and moved upcourt. As time ticked away, he fired up a shot from behind half-court . . . and it went in at the buzzer! Bulls 119, Lakers 117! It capped off a fantastic night for the Australian. He became the first player to have a triple-double AND a buzzer-beater against the Lakers in the same game.

The mighty Antetokounmpo (right) delivered an NBA Cup to Milwaukee.

Triple-Double: Two-time NBA MVP **Nikola Jokić** became just the third player ever to average a triple-double for a season. The Denver Nuggets star averaged 29.6 points, 12.7 rebounds, and 10.2 assists. He joins **Oscar Robertson** and **Russell Westbrook** in this small club. Westbrook also plays for Denver, and he and Jokić both had triple-doubles in the same game twice, a record for teammates. And a final, memorable Jokić stat: In a March game, he was the first player ever to have a 30/20/20 game, with 31 points, 21 rebounds, and 22 assists!

Jokić continues as an all-around star.

NBA Playoffs

Curry led the Warriors to a playoff upset.

- The LA Clippers nearly pulled an upset over the Denver Nuggets, taking them to seven games. But Denver's **Aaron Gordon** had 22 points to lead his team to a 120-101 Game 7 win.
- The LA Lakers were just too tired, it seemed. The team was forced to play its starting five for too many minutes, and the talented Timberwolves rolled over them in five games.
- Led by **"Playoff" Jimmy Butler** and hot-shooting **Stephen Curry**, the Warriors upset the No. 2 Houston Rockets in seven games. Curry had 22 points in the clinching win, while **Buddy Hield** poured in 9 three-pointers in a 103-89 win.
- In the first two games of the second round, the New York Knicks twice came from 20 points behind to beat the Boston Celtics. Then Boston lost star **Jayson Tatum** to an injury. That helped the Knicks win in six games, making it to their first Eastern Conference final in 25 seasons!
- After trading wins for the first four games, the Thunder and the Nuggets faced a key Game 5. **Shai Gilgeous-Alexander** poured in 31 points, and OKC won 112-105. Denver tied the series in Game 6, but in Game 7 the Thunder dominated, winning 125-93.
- Though the Cleveland Cavaliers finished atop the Eastern Conference with 64 wins, they were upset in the second round by the Indiana Pacers.

Eastern Conference Final

PACERS 4, KNICKS 2

The Knicks thought they had Game 1 in the bag, leading by 14 points with just over three minutes left. But the Pacers had other ideas. They charged back and tied the game with only seconds left. **Tyrese Haliburton**'s long shot hit the rim, bounced high in the air, and as Knicks fans held their breath . . . the ball fell into the basket. Indiana won 138-135 in overtime. The Knicks nearly had a comeback of their own in Game 2 but ran out of time and Indiana won 114-109, helped by **Pascal Siakam**'s 39 points. Then the Knicks returned the favor, beating the Pacers 106-100 to climb back into the series. **Karl-Anthony Towns** had 20 of his 24 points in the fourth quarter to lead the Knicks. In Game 6, the Pacers earned their first trip to the NBA Finals since 2000 with a 125-108 win. Siakam was named the series MVP.

Western Conference Final

THUNDER 4, TIMBERWOLVES 1

The Thunder had the NBA's best record in the regular season, and they looked like it in Games 1 and 2. **Gilgeous-Alexander** led the way with 31 and 38 points. OKC won each game by at least 15 points, continuing its playoff trend of big wins. Minnesota came back with a big 143-101 win in Game 3. **Anthony Edwards** had 30 points, and teammate **Julius Randle** added 24. OKC shook off the big loss and took a commanding 3-1 lead . . . but only by the very small margin of 128-126. In that Game 4 win, SGA continued his hot play with 40 points and kept it up with 34 more in Game 5. The Thunder smashed the Wolves 124-94 to reach their first Finals since 2012.

Shai Gilgeous-Alexander

2025 NBA Finals

Oklahoma City 4, Indiana 3

Haliburton's shot stunned OKC.

GAME 1
Indiana 111, Oklahoma City 110

How long do you have to lead a game before you win? It's not a trick question. The answer is—as long as you're ahead when it ends. The Pacers held the lead during this game for exactly 0.3 seconds . . . and won. The Thunder had dominated play, and were ahead by 15 points in the fourth quarter. With less than 90 seconds left, they still led by five. But a miss gave Indiana's **Tyrese Haliburton** the chance at one last shot. He buried it with those 0.3 seconds left to give Indiana its first lead. It was the fourth time in the playoffs that the Pacers had rallied from behind late in the game, and Haliburton had made clutch shots in all of those.

GAME 2
Oklahoma City 123, Indiana 107

A tough loss might have put some teams off their game. Not the Thunder. They bounced back as they have throughout the playoffs, smashing the Pacers by 16 points. There was no Indiana comeback this time, as OKC's star **Shai Gilgeous-Alexander** led the way, pouring in 34 points and dishing out 8 assists. It was his record-tying 11th game in this postseason with 30 and 5. During a big second quarter, the Thunder led by as many as 23 points.

GAME 3
Indiana 116, Oklahoma City 107

This game looked like it was going the Thunder's way, and they led by five going into the fourth quarter. But the Pacers' fans, all wearing matching yellow T-shirts, helped their team rally. Indiana outscored OKC 32-18 in the fourth quarter and won going away. The Pacers' depth was key. Their bench players outscored the Thunder's reserves 49-18, led by **Bennedict Mathurin**'s 27 points.

Williams went wild in Game 5.

GAME 4

Oklahoma City 111, Indiana 104

A close game came down to the final few minutes. The Thunder made the most of them while the Pacers went cold. Trailing late in the game, Oklahoma City went on a 12-1 run to take the lead and seal the victory. SGA poured in 35, including seven clutch free throws in the fourth quarter.

GAME 5

Oklahoma City 120, Indiana 109

A tough night for Haliburton (4 points) and an awesome night for **Jalen Williams** (40 points; only the third player under 25 years old to score that many in a Finals game) turned into a Thunder win. It was almost a big Indiana comeback. They were behind by 18 at one point, but that shrank to two points before OKC pulled away late. It was the first time since March 10 that the Pacers had lost back-to-back games.

GAME 6

Indiana 108, Oklahoma City 91

The Pacers just refused to lose at home. Though Haliburton was limping on an injured leg, he led the team to a surprising blowout of the Thunder to force Game 7. The Pacers played just too fast for the Thunder in this one, streaking down the court on fast break after fast break. By the third quarter, they were ahead by as many as 31 points. The Thunder scored its fewest points of the season, too!

GAME 7

Oklahoma City 103, Indiana 91

It figured that this tense series would come down to the wire. And it pretty much did. The Pacers led by just one at halftime. However, they had lost Haliburton to a leg injury. After the break, the Thunder just thundered. They outscored the Pacers by 14 points in the third quarter and cruised to victory. SGA was named the Finals MVP, matching his season award.

SGA = MVP x 2!

2024–25 NBA Stat Leaders

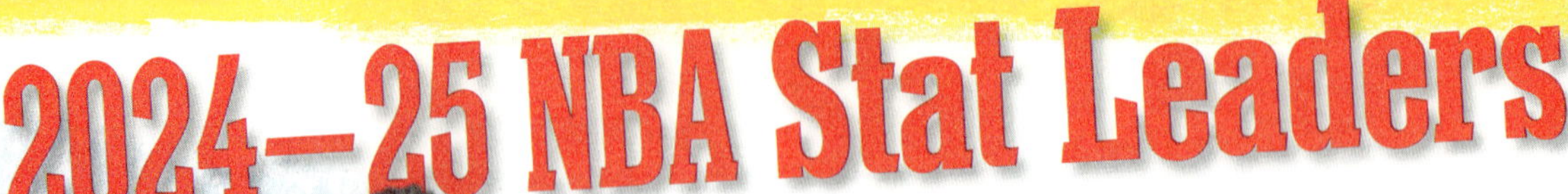

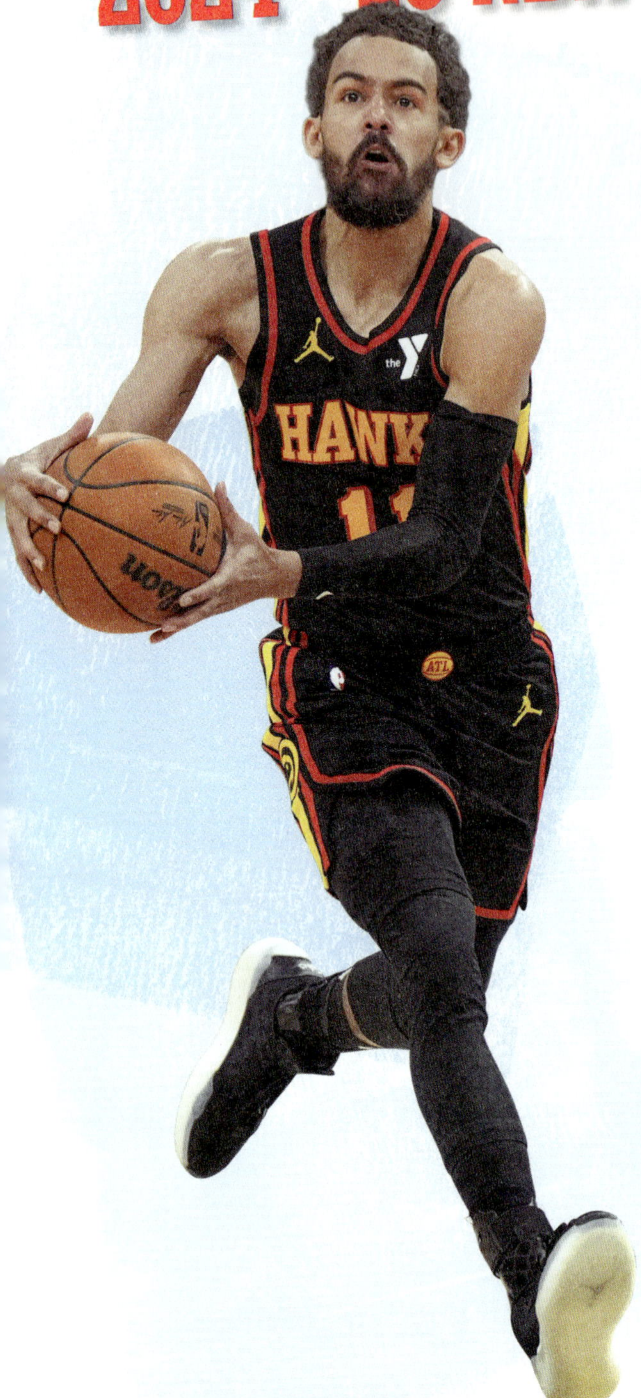

All stats are per-game averages except for total three-point baskets.

32.7 POINTS
Shai Gilgeous-Alexander
THUNDER

11.6 ASSISTS
Trae Young
HAWKS

13.9 REBOUNDS
Domantas Sabonis
KINGS

3.0 STEALS
Dyson Daniels
HAWKS

3.8 BLOCKS
Victor Wembanyama
SPURS

320 THREES
Anthony Edwards
TIMBERWOLVES

2024–25 NBA Awards

MOST VALUABLE PLAYER
SHAI GILGEOUS-ALEXANDER
THUNDER

DEFENSIVE PLAYER OF THE YEAR
EVAN MOBLEY▸▸▸
CAVALIERS

SIXTH MAN OF THE YEAR
PAYTON PRITCHARD
CELTICS

ROOKIE OF THE YEAR
STEPHON CASTLE
SPURS

MOST IMPROVED PLAYER
DYSON DANIELS
HAWKS

COACH OF THE YEAR
KENNY ATKINSON
CAVALIERS

COLLEGE BASKETBALL

YESSSSSS!
Connecticut's Jana El Alfy shows how all the Huskies feel after beating South Carolina 82-59 to win the NCAA championship. The Huskies moved pretty easily through the tournament to win their 12th title, the most of all-time in women's hoops. Read more about the rest of the women's college hoops season inside!

OH YEAH!

Florida head coach Todd Golden wears the net after his team won the men's NCAA championship. The Gators beat Houston in an exciting, down-to-the-wire final game 65-63. The whole men's season featured a lot of great teams, but only one could end up No. 1. Read all about it . . . just turn the page!

College Hoops

Iowa's **Caitlin Clark** was the big story in college basketball in 2023–24. Who would grab the headlines in 2024–25? On the women's side, megastar **Paige Bueckers** took center stage during her final season at Connecticut. For the men, Duke's **Cooper Flagg** played a bunch of games before turning 18 years old. His youth did not stop him from becoming the biggest name in the country. But there were lots more big names and big stories in college basketball!

Because so many colleges moved to new conferences, many teams were playing new opponents. (See our College Football section for more on the conference changes.) For example, UCLA had a Big Ten road trip that took them to Nebraska, Michigan, Maryland, and New Jersey all in one week. The ACC, SEC, and Big 12 also welcomed new teams and new rivalries.

Amid all the moving around, some of the men's usual top schools fell behind. Late in the regular season, six recent former champs were not even in the top 25. These included Baylor, Connecticut, Kansas, North Carolina, Villanova, and Virginia. Meanwhile, several high-ranked teams were chasing their school's first championship, such as Auburn, Alabama, and Houston. Five different teams held the number-one spot for at least a week, and 50 different teams earned votes in the season-long top 25.

On the women's side, many familiar teams remained among the best. Defending champ South Carolina was in it until the end, while Connecticut and Bueckers made the final again. Texas and LSU remained near the top, along

Cooper Flagg

with Notre Dame. However, two schools from the West, USC and UCLA, used their move to the Big Ten conference to make big leaps. UCLA made the first NCAA Final Four in its history. USC was led by national player of the year **JuJu Watkins**. Only her knee injury in a tournament game slowed down the Trojans' great season. Also, five different women's teams were ranked No. 1 in the national rankings during the regular season, the most in history.

At the end, the men's Final Four averaged more than 15.3 million viewers, with every eye in the nation glued on the championship game that came to the final possession! For the women, a clash of titans in the title game drew more than eight million views, the most for a non–Caitlin Clark game in women's basketball history!

No matter where college teams moved in their conferences, no one moved from the screen to watch two great championship games wrap up another exciting season!

Watkins was an all-around superstar.

AP TOP 10: MEN

1. Florida
2. Houston
3. Duke
4. Auburn
5. Tennessee
6. Alabama
7. Michigan State
8. Texas Tech
9. Maryland
10. Michigan

AP TOP 10: WOMEN

1. Connecticut
2. South Carolina
3. UCLA
4. Texas
5. USC
6. TCU
7. Duke
8. LSU
9. NC State
10. Notre Dame

Hoop Notes: Men

Big man Viktor Lakhin led Clemson's big win.

No Mercy in Missouri: Talk about mismatches! First, the University of Missouri–Kansas City beat Kansas Christian 124-36 on November 8. Then they whomped Calvary 119-19 ten days later. UMKC became the first team in NCAA Division I history to win two games by 85-plus points in the same season.

Self-Help: On November 12, the Kansas Jayhawks defeated Michigan State 77-69. That gave coach **Bill Self** his 591st win at Kansas, the most in program history. A week after that, he became the 30th coach in NCAA men's basketball history to win 800 total games. He was still not number one among active coaches, though. Arkansas coach **John Calipari** ended the season with 855 wins.

Here to Stay: After winning back-to-back national titles, Connecticut coach **Dan Hurley** had a chance to make the leap to the NBA. The Los Angeles Lakers, led by "the King," **LeBron James**, offered Hurley their coaching job. But Connecticut gave Hurley 50 million reasons (dollars!) to stay where he was. On opening night, Huskies fans showered Hurley with applause as their team hung its second championship banner in a row.

A Bahamas Buzzer-Beater: Two top-25 teams met early in the season, and their game had a wild finish. No. 13 Baylor faced No. 22 St. John's in the Bahamas. Baylor trailed by as many as 18 points but came back to tie the game and force overtime. In the final second of the second OT period, Baylor's **Jeremy Roach** buried a buzzer-beater to give his team a 99-98 win.

2,000 for Temple: On December 18, Temple edged out a 62-61 win against Davidson, making them just the sixth D-I school with 2,000 wins. Not even one month later, Syracuse made it seven with its 2,000th win, which came over Georgia Tech. The two schools joined these other famous programs in the 2,000-W Club: Kansas, Kentucky, North Carolina, Duke, and UCLA.

Teenage Star: **Cooper Flagg** came to Duke expected to be a young superstar. In fact, he did not even turn 18 years old until he had already played a dozen games for the Blue Devils. But he went way past the hype. One example? He set an ACC freshman record with 42 points in a win over Notre Dame. That was one of Flagg's great games on his way to picking up a stack of player-of-the-year awards.

Shaken Up: That's what the national rankings were after games on February 8. No. 1 Auburn fell to No. 6 Florida 90-81. **Walter Clayton Jr.** had 19 points for Florida, while teammate **Alex Condon** had a double-double (17 points, 10 rebounds). It was the first time the Gators had beaten a top-ranked team on the road. No. 2 Duke lost as well! Duke was on a 16-game winning streak, but that ended with a 77-71 Clemson win. **Viktor Lakhin** led the way with 22 points.

What a Game! When two top-10 teams meet, fans hope that they get to watch a thriller. They got their wish when No. 5 Tennessee battled No. 6 Alabama. Alabama led late in the game, but Tennessee scored seven points in the final 30 seconds while allowing Bama zero. The capper was a buzzer-beating, three-point basket by Tennessee's **Jahmai Mashack** to clinch a 79-76 win.

Shot of the Year?: What an ending to the Michigan State–Maryland game! The two teams were both ranked in the top 20 and were in a defensive battle. With just a few seconds left and the score tied 55-55, Maryland missed a shot. Michigan State's **Tre Holloman** grabbed the ball, dribbled once, and launched a shot from beyond half-court. It went in!

Check the clock: Mashack at the buzzer!

Hoop Notes: Women

Geno Stands Alone: Coach **Geno Auriemma** set a new record for victories on November 20, 2024. His Connecticut team beat Fairleigh Dickinson 85-41. It was his 1,217th win, moving him past women's all-time leader **Tara VanDerveer**. Auriemma has led UConn since the 1985–86 season and has had only one losing record . . . in that first season! He ended the 2024–25 season with 1,250 career wins.

But He Didn't Win Them All: The USC Trojans were one of the big stories of the season. On December 21, they beat powerhouse Connecticut for the first time ever, 72-70. **JuJu Watkins** led the way with 25 points. UConn rallied from 18 points behind to make it close, but Watkins sealed the win with clutch late free throws.

Latson poured in points for FSU.

Scoring Champ: Florida State had a pretty successful season, partly thanks to the the nation's top scorer. Junior guard **Ta'Niya Latson** averaged 25.2 points per game. Her biggest game came January 2 against Virginia Tech, when Latson scored 40 points. It was one of eight games in which Latson scored at least 30, making her must-see TV for Seminoles fans.

USC RUNS LA: That's what the USC Trojans wrote on their social media pages after they dismantled No. 1 UCLA 71-60 on February 13. It was the Trojans' first win over a No. 1 opponent since 1983. Watkins had her biggest game of the season with 38 points, 11 rebounds, and 8 blocks. The Trojans were also the first team to beat UCLA in 2024–25.

New Frosh Star: In a 98-88 overtime win over Auburn, **Mikayla Blakes** had more than half of Vanderbilt's points! Blakes poured in 55 to set a new all-time record for a freshman

Betts made sure UCLA was a winner.

Division I player. She made 15 baskets, including a pair of three-pointers, and was 23-of-24 from the free throw line. She had 53 in a game earlier in the season, too!

No More Home Streak: Heading into the February 16 battle between No. 4 South Carolina and No. 7 Connecticut, the Gamecocks had not lost at home for 71 straight games. That streak ended with an 87-58 Huskies win, led by **Azzi Fudd**'s 28 points. Superstar **Paige Bueckers** also had a great all-around game for UConn. She recorded a double-double, with 12 points and 10 assists, plus 7 rebounds.

New Kids on the Block: UCLA and USC not only joined the Big Ten in 2024–25 . . . they dominated! Most of the schools in this conference are in the Midwest, while these two schools are near the Pacific Ocean in Los Angeles! No matter where they went to class, UCLA and USC were the best in the conference. The Bruins won the Big Ten championship game over the Trojans, led by star **Lauren Betts**. She was named the Big Ten Tournament's Most Outstanding Player. The six-foot-seven center not only averaged more than 20 points per game this season but also set a new school record with 100 blocked shots.

Big Sky, Big Moment: After watching the Montana State Bobcats go 17–1 in conference play, the Montana Grizzlies had their chance to turn the tables in the Big Sky championship. Montana led 57-56 in the game's final seconds. But then Montana State's **Marah Dykstra** tipped in a basket at the buzzer to win 58-57. The shocking win sent the Bobcats to the NCAA tournament for the first time since 2022.

Dykstra's big play saved the day!

Men's NCAA Highlights

Christian Shumate helped McNeese win.

SOUTHLAND STANDS UP

No. 12–seed McNeese State, of the Southland Conference, enjoyed its second NCAA tournament appearance in a row by upsetting No. 5 Clemson 69-67 in the first round. McNeese nearly blew a 31-13 lead in the second half, but the Cowboys had just enough to break the Tigers' hearts. It was the first NCAA tournament victory for McNeese State (which is in Louisiana) in its 52-year Division I history.

RAMS' HOUSE!

The Colorado State Rams joined the 12-over-5 upset party when they beat Memphis 78-70 in the first round. That sent the Rams to the second round for the first time in 12 seasons. **Kyan Evans** scored 23 points and made a CSU tournament-record six three-pointers in the win.

RAZOR-SHARP

One of the biggest second-round upsets came when No. 10 Arkansas knocked off No. 2 St. John's 75-66. The win sent the Razorbacks to their 15th Sweet Sixteen, while St. John's fell one win shy of setting a new program record for wins in a single season.

NO THREE-PEAT

Connecticut came into the tournament as the two-time defending national champ. Their dream of a "three-peat" ended in the second round. UConn fell to eventual champion, Florida, 77-75.

D.J. Wagner and Arkansas had a big W.

Tick-tick-tick . . . Queen shoots! **BZZZZ!**

Connecticut was ahead as many as six points in the final 10 minutes. But **Walter Clayton Jr.**'s 23 points pushed the Gators to his team's first Sweet Sixteen since 2017.

HAIL MARYLAND

Colorado State came oh-so-close to another upset win but had their dream ended by No. 4 Maryland. **Derik Queen** muscled his way to a last-second, season-saving bucket to give Maryland a 72-71 win. It was the first buzzer-beater in the men's tournament since the Final Four in 2023. It also sent the Terps to their first Sweet Sixteen in nine years.

A SWEET THRILLER

Perhaps the best game of the Sweet Sixteen was the 62-60 win by Houston over Purdue. It was a back-and-forth battle from the start, with Houston clinging to a lead most of the way. However, with 33 seconds left, Purdue finally tied the game 60-60 on a **Camden Heide** three-pointer. **Milos Uzan** of Houston then missed a go-ahead shot, but the rebound was knocked out of bounds by Purdue. On the in-bounds play with 2.8 seconds left, Uzan passed to **Joseph Tugler**, who immediately returned the ball to Uzan, who dropped it in the basket for the winning points.

NO. 1S ALL AROUND

For the first time since 2008, all four No. 1 seeds advanced to the Final Four. Auburn was the last No. 1 to make it in, holding on to beat Michigan State 70-64. Star forward **Johni Broome** was the key, putting up his 21st double-double of the season (25 points and 14 rebounds).

Florida's Clayton battled at the basket in the semifinal game against Auburn.

Men's Final Four

NATIONAL SEMIFINALS

Florida 79, Auburn 73

The Auburn Tigers led by nine points at halftime. Could they cruise to victory? Not while **Walter Clayton Jr.** was on Florida! He scored 34 points to lead the Gators to the win. Clayton became the first player since Hall of Famer **Larry Bird** in 1979 to have back-to-back 30-point games in the Elite Eight and Final Four. Florida's defense helped a lot, too. After a 46-point first half, Auburn was held to just 27 points in the final period. The win sent the Gators to the title game for the first time since they won it all in 2007.

Houston 70, Duke 67

A comeback for the ages sent the Houston Cougars to their first title game since 1984 and prevented the Duke Blue Devils from advancing to their 12th in program history. Duke led by as many as 14 points with under 12 minutes remaining, but the Blue Devils made just one field goal in the final 10 minutes and 30 seconds of action. A second-half surge from Houston's **L.J. Cryer** and company ended with a 9-0 run over the final 33 seconds. It was one of the biggest comebacks in Final Four history.

Championship Game

Florida 65, Houston 63

For the first time in 18 years, the Florida Gators were the last team dancing. The final was a comeback that fans will be talking about for years. Florida trailed by as many as 12 points early in the second half. One reason was that Gators star **Walter Clayton Jr.** was held scoreless for the entire first half. In the second half, however, Clayton came through with 11 points, including a three-point play that tied the game at 48-48.

The game was close the rest of the way, but Houston seemed in control. They held off rally after rally. But Florida kept chipping away, and Houston had trouble finding good shots to take. With less than a a minute left, Florida got the lead for the first time since the early minutes. **Alijah Martin** made two free throws to put the Gators ahead 64-63.

Still, even then, Houston had a chance to score but lost the ball on a turnover and gave up another free throw. But they still had one final time with the ball. They tried to find a way through the tough Florida defense, led by Clayton. A Houston player jumped to make a shot, but could not get the shot off. He had to drop the ball (otherwise, it would have been a traveling call). Players dived to the floor after the bouncing ball, and Florida's **Alex Condon** gobbled it up safely as the buzzer sounded!

In just his third year, Florida's **Todd Golden** became the youngest coach to win a title since 1983. It was also the first championship for the SEC since 2012. Golden and the Gators will enter 2025–26 looking to win back-to-back titles just like Florida did in 2006 and 2007.

When Condon snagged this loose ball, Florida's championship was decided!

Women's NCAA Highlights

JUMPIN' JACKRABBITS!

For the first time since 1994—when this tournament grew to 64 teams—no teams seeded higher than 10th moved past the first round. One of the two 10 seeds that did was the South Dakota State Jackrabbits. They upset 7-seed Oklahoma State 74-68.

Jaquez's three-pointer sealed the UCLA win.

Paige Meyer made key shots for SDSU.

QUACKIN' DUCKS!

No. 7–seed Vanderbilt thought they may have saved their season when they came from 19 points behind to force overtime against No. 10 Oregon. Instead, the Ducks kicked back into gear, coming away with the upset after winning 77-73.

QUICK EXIT

Arkansas State was thrilled to make its first NCAA tournament appearance. They were not so thrilled to face 1-seed and 11-time champion Connecticut in the first round. UConn showed the Arkansas

State players how it was done, winning 103-34. At least Arkansas State got to say they played against the champs!

SAD INJURY

The basketball world had its heart broken on March 24 when **JuJu Watkins** badly hurt her knee in USC's second-round game against Mississippi State. Watkins's team rallied to beat Mississippi State, but the Trojans were left without their best player from then on. They lost in the Elite Eight to Connecticut.

WHAT A GAME!

Alabama and Maryland put on an entertaining show in the second round. Bama's **Sarah Ashlee Barker** led the way with 45 points, one of the best single games in tournament history. Maryland's **Shyanne Sellers** led her squad with 28. Sellers got just a little more help, and her Terps won 111-108 in double OT to reach their fourth Sweet Sixteen in five years.

DEFENSE! DEFENSE!

In an Elite Eight matchup, No. 1–seed UCLA drew 3-seed LSU. LSU's **Flau'jae Johnson** had 28 points to lead all scorers in the game. But a second-half defensive change for the Bruins helped them return to the Final Four. UCLA's **Gabriela Jaquez** put the game on ice with a late three-pointer in the 72-65 win.

FIVE FOR "FOUR"

Defending champ South Carolina kept its repeat dreams alive and advanced to their fifth-straight Final Four. They slipped by 2-seed Duke 54-50. In the final 30 seconds, Duke actually had a chance to steal one from the Gamecocks, but a stop and a successful trip to the free throw line kept South Carolina on the dance floor.

TEXAS TWO-STEP

Texas and TCU are longtime rivals in many sports. They met in an Elite Eight game to add another page to their rivalry. In the end, it was the Texas defense that sent their team to its first Final Four in 22 years. The Longhorns held the Horned Frogs to 27 percent shooting. Though TCU superstar **Hailey Van Lith** scored 17 points in her final collegiate game, it was not enough, and Texas won 58-47.

Barker of Bama had a big, big day!

Women's Final Four

NATIONAL SEMIFINALS

The all-around game of Edwards led the way.

Connecticut 85, UCLA 51

The Huskies' 34-point win was the largest margin of victory in women's Final Four history. Superstar **Paige Bueckers** had "only" 16 points in her last semifinal for Connecticut. But she had a lot of help. Freshman **Sarah Strong** scored 22 points. Senior star **Azzi Fudd** had 19. UCLA's star center **Lauren Betts** did all she could, scoring 26 points. Connecticut headed to its record 13th NCAA title game.

Strong was just that in the Huskies' win.

South Carolina 74, Texas 57

These two top seeds went toe-to-toe with a trip to the title game on the line. Texas jumped out to an early 10-2 lead. By halftime, South Carolina had a 38-35 lead they would never give up. It was the fourth time that the two schools met this season, and SC won three of those. Both teams got strong games from players off the bench. Texas was led by **Jordan Lee**'s 16 points. South Carolina's **Joyce Edwards** had 13 points and 11 rebounds for a double-double. The win sent head coach **Dawn Staley** to the championship game in search of a second-straight title and a fourth overall.

National Championship

Connecticut 82, South Carolina 59

In the first quarter, South Carolina looked up and saw that they were ahead 11-8. Could the defending champs win back-to-back titles? Well, it was nice while it lasted. Connecticut ended the first quarter on a 6-0 run, took the lead in the game, and never looked back. After three quarters, UConn led 62-42. Ten minutes later, coach **Geno Auriemma**'s dynasty continued with UConn winning the 12th national title in program history and first since 2016. The winning margin was tied for the third-largest in championship game history behind two other Connecticut wins (2013 and 2016). UConn's big three of **Azzi Fudd**, **Sarah Strong**, and **Paige Bueckers** combined for 65 points. Those three alone outscored the Gamecocks by six points! Fudd, who had 24 points, was named the tournament's Most Outstanding Player.

Azzi Fudd

"As a great teammate, a great leader. I think those are the two most important things to me, being somebody that people love to play with . . . and who wears a UConn jersey with pride."

— PAIGE BUECKERS ON HOW SHE WANTS TO BE REMEMBERED

ICE HOCKEY

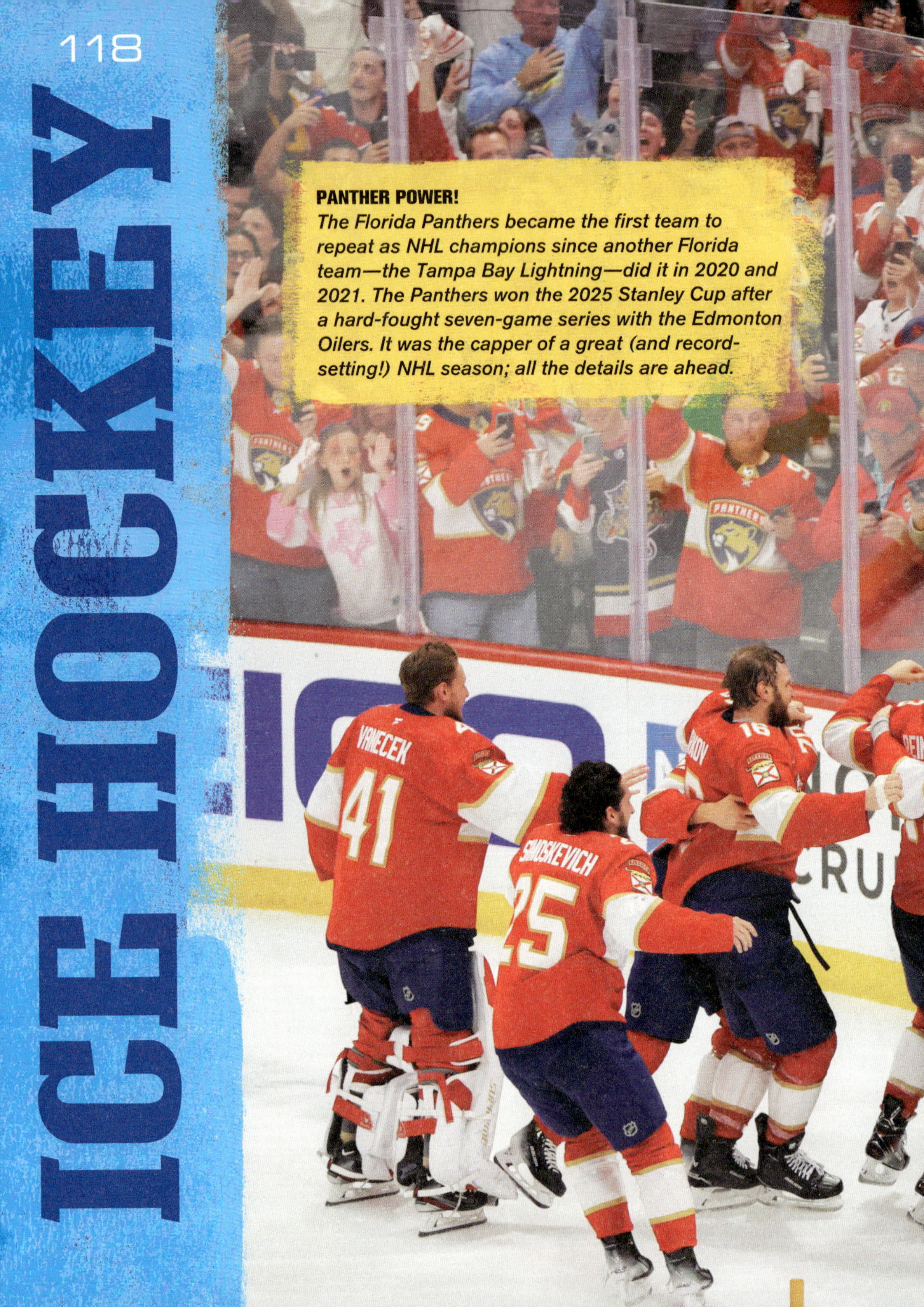

PANTHER POWER!
The Florida Panthers became the first team to repeat as NHL champions since another Florida team—the Tampa Bay Lightning—did it in 2020 and 2021. The Panthers won the 2025 Stanley Cup after a hard-fought seven-game series with the Edmonton Oilers. It was the capper of a great (and record-setting!) NHL season; all the details are ahead.

DITTO TIMES TWO
Just like in the NHL, the PWHL had a repeat champion. The Minnesota Frost won their second-straight league title, beating the Ottawa Charge in the Walter Cup series. The PWHL is making news in 2026, too; see page 128 for more!

NHL 2024–25

The biggest news in hockey in the 2024–25 season was the biggest number . . . of goals, that is. Hockey's most famous record fell this season when **Alexander Ovechkin** of the Washington Capitals passed **Wayne Gretzky**'s mark of 894 career goals. Ovechkin scored number 895 on April 6 against the New York Islanders. "Ovi" ended the season with 897, and he says he'll be back with the Capitals in 2025–26 to push that number even higher.

Overall, it was a season of great performances. Colorado Avalanche star **Cale Makar** became the first defenseman to get 30 goals and 60 assists in one season since **Paul Coffey** did it in 1989.

Coach Campbell was on the bench for Seattle.

Sergei Bobrovsky of the Florida Panthers became the fastest goalie in NHL history to reach 400 wins. Fellow netminder **Andrei Vasilevskiy** of the Tampa Bay Lightning was the fastest to reach 300 wins.

Sidney Crosby of the Pittsburgh Penguins broke another of the great Gretzky's records when he made it 20 seasons with an average of at least one point per game. Gretzky did it in 19 seasons.

A hockey tradition changed this season when former Canadian national team standout **Jessica Campbell** was named assistant coach for the Seattle Kraken. She became the first female bench coach in the NHL.

The Utah Hockey Club, which moved north from Arizona, was cheered on by a sold-out crowd every night in their new Salt Lake City arena. After their season was over, they revealed their new name: Utah Mammoth.

Rookies **Lane Hutson** in Montreal and

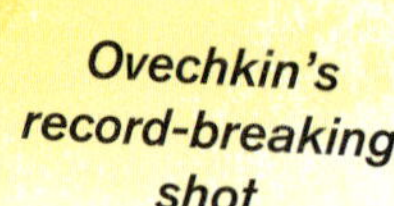

Ovechkin's record-breaking shot

Macklin Celebrini in San Jose lifted their teams with their amazing skills. Huston became just the ninth rookie in NHL history (and only the second defenseman) with 60 assists in a single season. On April 19, Celebrini scored a hat trick and had two assists to notch five points—setting a team record for an 18-year-old.

The Columbus Blue Jackets faced a terrible loss. Left winger **Johnny Gaudreau** was killed over the summer, along with his brother, when both were struck by a drunk driver. The team, which had finished at the bottom of the Eastern Conference in 2024, rallied around Gaudreau's memory and made a mighty push for the playoffs. They almost got in but were edged out by the Canadiens.

As the season wound down, the Capitals and the Jets jockeyed for the Presidents' Trophy (the team with the most points overall). In the end, Winnipeg grabbed the prize for the first time in team history, led by their goalie **Connor Hellebuyck**, who topped the NHL in wins (47), shutouts (8), and goals-against average (2.00).

2024–25 FINAL STANDINGS

EASTERN CONFERENCE		WESTERN CONFERENCE	
TEAM	**POINTS**	**TEAM**	**POINTS**
CAPITALS	111	JETS	116
MAPLE LEAFS	108	GOLDEN KNIGHTS	110
LIGHTNING	102	STARS	106
HURRICANES	99	KINGS	105
PANTHERS	98	AVALANCHE	102
SENATORS	97	OILERS	101
DEVILS	91	WILD	97
CANADIENS	91	BLUES	96
BLUE JACKETS	89	FLAMES	96
RED WINGS	86	CANUCKS	90
RANGERS	85	HOCKEY CLUB	89
ISLANDERS	82	DUCKS	80
PENGUINS	80	KRAKEN	76
SABRES	79	PREDATORS	68
BRUINS	76	BLACKHAWKS	61
FLYERS	76	SHARKS	52

As always in the NHL, the regular season set the stage for the exciting playoffs. Fans enjoyed some amazing games and series. In the end, Canadian fans were disappointed, while Florida fans were roaring!

A Fabulous 4 Nations!

Instead of a single All-Star Game, the NHL held a four-team mini tournament. The 4 Nations Face-Off featured national teams from the USA, Canada, Sweden, and Finland. NHL players love to compete for their country, and the three-game round-robin play was filled with hard hitting and plenty of scoring. Two-thirds of the 4 Nations players ended up in the 2025 Stanley Cup playoffs.

The United States and Canada faced off in the final game. It was an exciting, gritty game that was tied 2-2 at the end of regulation. A little more than eight minutes into OT, **Connor** beat **Connor**, as **McDavid** fired the puck past **Hellebuyck** to win the tournament for Canada.

2025 NHL Playoffs

No lead was safe in the 2025 playoffs, as multiple-goal leads were wiped out in the final seconds and series leads were erased. Here are some highlights.

Late-Game Magic

In the first round, the Blues faced the Jets, who finished with the best record in the NHL. In the deciding Game 7, the Blues had a two-goal lead with less than two minutes left. The Jets cut the lead to 3-2 when **Vladislav Namestnikov** scored. Then, with just 2.2 seconds on the clock, **Cole Perfetti** tipped home a shot to tie the score! It was the latest game-tying goal in a Game 7 in NHL history. The Jets' **Adam Lowry** finally netted the winner at 16:10 of the second overtime.

Comeback Time

Florida almost didn't make it to the Stanley Cup Final. They trailed the Toronto Maple Leafs by two games and were losing Game 3. Then the Panthers scratched back and forced overtime. **Brad Marchand** scored the OT winner for Florida. It was Marchand's fourth career playoff overtime goal. After the two teams tied at 3–3 in games, the Panthers crushed the Leafs 6-1 to clinch the series.

Dancing in Dallas

The Stars beat the Jets in Game 1 of the second round. The big shots were three straight goals by **Mikko Rantanen**. After Winnipeg won Game 2, Rantanen did it again—he had a goal and two assists in a 5-2 Dallas win. **Mikael Granlund** scored all three goals in Dallas' Game 4 win, to give the Stars a 3–1 series lead. After Jets star goalie **Connor Hellyebuck** blanked the Stars 4-0, Dallas sent the Jets home on an overtime goal from Thomas Harley in Game 6. The Jets' loss made them the ninth Presidents' Trophy winner in 10 years not to make it out of the second round.

Perfetti (91) tipped in the tying goal in the nick of time—just 2.2 seconds left!

McDavid got past all the Stars to net this breathtaking Game 5 goal.

EASTERN CONFERENCE FINAL

PANTHERS 4, HURRICANES 1

The Florida Panthers and Carolina Hurricanes met in the Eastern Conference Final for the second time in three seasons. The Panthers mauled the Hurricanes, winning the series in five games. The Panthers dominated with their great forechecking and balanced scoring. That balance showed in the final game. Five different Panthers scored to clinch the series. Florida became the ninth team to reach three Stanley Cup finals in a row.

WESTERN CONFERENCE FINAL

OILERS 4, STARS 1

The Dallas Stars shone brightly in Game 1. Down by two goals, they scored three in the third period to take the lead. They won 6-3. Oilers goalie **Stuart Skinner** then shut the door by allowing only two goals in the next three games, all Edmonton victories. In Game 5, Dallas gave up three goals in the first eight minutes. But they battled back to pull within one. Then the Oilers' sensational center **Connor McDavid** answered with a dazzling breakaway goal that proved to be the game and series winner. Edmonton advanced to the Stanley Cup final for a rematch with Florida.

Carter Verhaeghe scored for Florida in Game 5.

2025 Stanley Cup Final

Florida Panthers 4, Edmonton Oilers 2

Draisaitl's Game 1 goal won it in OT.

GAME 1

Oilers 4, Panthers 3 (OT)

Edmonton fans were barely in their seats before **Leon Draisaitl** had them standing when he scored just 1:06 into the game. Florida went ahead in the second period, but early in the third, Edmonton's **Mattias Ekholm** tied the game. In overtime, the Oilers earned a power play. **Connor McDavid** floated a gorgeous pass to Draisaitl, who buried a shot, giving Edmonton the win.

GAME 2

Panthers 5, Oilers 4 (2 OT)

Both teams scored early, and the game was tied when McDavid made magic. He gave Edmonton the lead by stickhandling past and through two defenders. Then he zipped a perfect pass to Draisaitl, who flipped the puck into the net. The Panthers battled back with two goals to take the lead late in the game. With only 18 seconds left, Florida's **Corey Perry** swatted home a loose puck to tie the score. In the second overtime, the Panthers' **Brad Marchand** slipped the puck under Oilers goalie **Stuart Skinner** on a breakaway for the game-winning goal.

GAME 3

Panthers 6, Oilers 1

There was no stopping Marchand, as he scored just 56 seconds into the game. **Carter Verhaeghe**'s laser shot over Skinner's shoulder gave the Panthers a two-goal lead. Edmonton scored, but Florida scored three of its goals thanks in part to 11 Oilers penalties.

GAME 4

Oilers 5, Panthers 4 (OT)

The Panthers pounced with three first-period goals, but the Oilers fought back in the second period to tie the score. In a tense third period, a Panthers turnover resulted in an Edmonton blast by **Jake Walman** to give the Oilers their first lead of the game. Then the Panthers' **Sam Reinhart** scored with 20 seconds left! But in overtime, Draisaitl scored his fourth overtime goal in the playoffs for the win.

GAME 5

Panthers 5, Oilers 2

Sam Bennett and Marchand got the Panthers off to a big start with two goals.

Three against one! Marchand finds a way through the Oilers for a Game 5 goal.

Then Marchand made a sensational play, weaving through Edmonton defenders, to make the score 3-0. McDavid scored his first goal of the series to chip at the Panthers' lead, but less than a minute later Reinhart fired home a goal.

Reinhart celebrates one of his four goals.

GAME 6

Panthers 5, Oilers 1

By the end of the second period the Panthers were ahead 3-0. In a last-ditch effort to close the gap, the Oilers pulled Skinner with less than seven minutes left. That let Reinhart score two empty-net goals. He ended up with four goals in the game, only the second player ever to do that while clinching a series. His teammate Bennett was awarded the Conn Smythe Trophy as playoffs MVP. After the game, Panthers captain **Aleksander Barkov** made sure that after he carried the Stanley Cup that it was handed off to every first-time Cup winner on the Panthers. Nice job, Cap!

2024–25 NHL Leaders

121 POINTS
Nikita Kucherov, Lightning

92 POINTS (DEFENSEMAN)
Cale Makar, Avalanche

52 GOALS
Leon Draisaitl, Oilers

84 ASSISTS
Nathan MacKinnon, Avalanche

◀◀◀ **Nikita Kucherov**, Lightning

+43 PLUS-MINUS
Ryan McDonagh, Lightning

17 POWER-PLAY GOALS
Jake Guentzel, Lightning

2.00 GOALS AGAINST AVG.
47 WINS
Connor Hellebuyck, Jets

.926 SAVE PCT.
Anthony Stolarz, Maple Leafs

1,584 SAVES
Igor Shesterkin, Rangers

2025 NHL Awards

Hart Memorial Trophy
MOST VALUABLE PLAYER
Vezina Trophy
TOP GOALTENDER
CONNOR HELLEBUYCK, JETS

James Norris Memorial Trophy
TOP DEFENSEMAN
CALE MAKAR, COLORADO

Calder Memorial Trophy
ROOKIE OF THE YEAR
LANE HUTSON, MONTREAL

Ted Lindsay Award
MOST OUTSTANDING PLAYER, VOTED BY THE NHL PLAYERS' ASSOCIATION
NIKITA KUCHEROV, LIGHTNING

Lady Byng Memorial Trophy
SPORTSMANSHIP
ANZE KOPITAR, KINGS

Jack Adams Award
COACH OF THE YEAR
SPENCER CARBERY, CAPITALS

Frank J. Selke Trophy
BEST DEFENSIVE FORWARD
King Clancy Memorial Trophy
LEADERSHIP ON AND OFF THE ICE
ALEKSANDER BARKOV, ▶▶▶ PANTHERS

Bill Masterton Memorial Trophy
PERSEVERANCE, SPORTSMANSHIP
SEAN MONAHAN, BLUE JACKETS

PWHL 2025

The second season of the Professional Women's Hockey League (PWHL) started with new names and logos for all six teams. The league also had a bigger season—30 games, up from 24. And the fans responded: In the first period of the Detroit game (between the New York Sirens and the Minnesota Frost), the league announced that more than one million fans had attended PWHL games to that point.

The schedule also included nine games played in arenas that were not part of the six teams. It was a way to let more fans check out the action. Fans of women's hockey in Denver set an attendance record of 14,018, which was soon broken by 14,288 fans in Detroit. In addition, hundreds of girls' hockey players played in clinics and met PWHL athletes.

Fillier was named Rookie of the Year.

The season featured a couple of red-hot rookies. Ottawa Charge goaltender **Gwyneth Philips** set a college save percentage record of .958 at Northeastern. The other top newcomer was former Princeton star **Sarah Fillier** of the New York Sirens. She ended her rookie season tied with hockey legend **Hilary Knight** of Boston for the most points with 29. She also tied Toronto superstar **Renata Fast** with 16 assists, and was named the Rookie of the Year. Although New York fell to last place in the league,

PLAYING THE WORLD

Fifty-seven PWHL players played in the IIHF Women's World Championship in Czechia in April. The league had players from seven of the ten countries. With 17 players, the Toronto Sceptres sent the most to the event. The Boston Fleet and Montreal Victoire each sent squad members to five different nations!

The United States won their 11th world title with a 4-3 overtime win against Canada. **Tessa Janecke** of Penn State scored the winning goal after a perfect feed from **Taylor Heise** of the Frost during the first overtime.

STAT LEADERS

29 POINTS
HILARY KNIGHT, BOSTON ▸▸▸
SARAH FILLIER, NEW YORK

19 GOALS
MARIE-PHILIP POULIN, MONTREAL

16 ASSISTS
SARAH FILLIER, NEW YORK
RENATA FAST, TORONTO

+17 PLUS-MINUS
MARIE-PHILIP POULIN, MONTREAL

22 POINTS, DEFENSE
SOPHIE JAQUES, MINNESOTA
RENATA FAST, TORONTO

1.86 GOALS AGAINST AVG.
0.932 SAVE PERCENTAGE
15 WINS
ANN-RENÉE DESBIENS, MONTREAL

young star Fillier gives fans a lot to look forward to in 2026.

The race to the playoffs was intense. With three games remaining in the regular season, only the Montreal Victoire had locked down their playoff spot. The Sceptres were the next team in, when they beat New York. The Charge clinched a spot when they won their last game in overtime against Toronto. Defending Walter Cup champion Minnesota also squeaked in on their last game, eliminating the Boston Fleet.

The top four teams—Montreal, Toronto, Ottawa, and Minnesota—headed for a two-round, best-of-five playoff tournament for the Walter Cup. The PWHL lets the No. 1 team pick who it will play in the first round. Montreal chose Ottawa. Did it work out?

Later, with every Cup Final game going to overtime, it turned out to be a great way to wrap up a successful second PWHL season. And there's more on the way in 2026, when two new teams in Vancouver and Seattle will join the PWHL. Women's hockey is on the move!

PWHL STANDINGS

TEAM	POINTS
Montreal **VICTOIRE**	53
Toronto **SCEPTRES**	48
Ottawa **CHARGE**	44
Minnesota **FROST**	44
Boston **FLEET**	44
New York **SIRENS**	37

PWHL Playoffs

Dubois (left) finally put in the Game 2 OT winner.

Minnesota 3, Toronto 1

Julia Gosling of Toronto scored twice in her playoff debut, leading her team to a 3-2 Game 1 win. **Lee Stecklein** of the Frost struck back in Game 2, scoring two goals and adding an assist to help the Frost to a 5-3 win and even the series. Minnesota defeated Toronto 7-5 in the highest-scoring game in PWHL history. The Frost booked their trip to the Final in Game 4, with a 4-3 overtime win. **Taylor Heise** scored the overtime winner.

Ottawa 3, Montreal 1

In the PWHL, the season's top finisher gets to pick their first-round opponent. Montreal chose third-place Ottawa—a team they beat in four of their six regular-season games. In their first playoff game in team history, Ottawa skated to a 3-2 victory. The Victoire got their first playoff win in Game 2, which became the longest in league history. Ottawa scored two goals in the third period to tie the game and force overtime. After two overtimes, Ottawa trainers taped packs of mustard to the bench, which the tired players ate to avoid cramps. The game finally ended in the fourth overtime after more than 135 minutes (more than two regular games!). Montreal's **Catherine Dubois** scored the game-winner. After recovering, the teams met again in Game 3, when Ottawa shut out Montreal 1-0. The Charge finished the job in Game 4 with a 2-1 win.

2025 PWHL AWARDS

BILLIE JEAN KING MVP AWARD
Marie-Philip Poulin, MONTREAL

DEFENDER OF THE YEAR
Renata Fast, TORONTO

GOALTENDER OF THE YEAR
Ann-Renée Desbiens, MONTREAL

ROOKIE OF THE YEAR
Sarah Fillier, NEW YORK

COACH OF THE YEAR
Kori Cheverie, MONTREAL

"HOCKEY FOR ALL" AWARD
Laura Stacey, MONTREAL

Walter Cup Final

Minnesota 3, Ottawa 1

The Frost piled on after capturing the Walter Cup again.

GAME 1

Ottawa 2, Minnesota 1 (OT)

The Charge took charge in overtime, when **Emily Clark** snapped the puck into the net three minutes in. The victory gave Ottawa a perfect 3-0 on home ice so far in the playoffs. The Frost had never won Game 1 of a playoff series in four attempts.

GAME 2

Minnesota 2, Ottawa 1 (OT)

Ottawa outshot Minnesota 38 to 24, but the game nearly ended in a scoreless tie. Charge defender **Jocelyne Larocque** scored with just 2:35 left in the third period. But with 15 seconds left in regulation, Minnesota's **Britta Curl-Salemme** scored the equalizer to send the game to overtime. She scored again in OT, handing Ottawa its first postseason loss.

GAME 3

Minnesota 2, Ottawa 1 (3 OT)

It was another low-scoring duel as **Maddie Rooney** made 35 saves for Minnesota and **Gwyneth Philips** stopped 45 shots for Ottawa. Charge forward Clark tapped a bouncing puck in halfway through the first period, then Frost defender **Lee Stecklein** tied the game with a shot from the blue line. The score remained 1-1 through the first overtime period and the second. Finally, at 9:57 of the third OT, **Katy Knoll** flicked in a quick backhand shot for the winning goal.

GAME 4

Minnesota 2, Ottawa 1 (OT)

With Minnesota up 1-0, Ottawa's **Tereza Vanišová** scored midway through the third period to tie the game at 1-1. For the fourth straight contest, the teams needed overtime. Twelve minutes into the first OT period, Game 3 hero Knoll passed to **Liz Schepers** in front of the net. Philips stopped the shot, but Schepers poked home the rebound. That won the game and clinched back-to-back Walter Cup titles for the Frost. Philips, Ottawa's rookie goaltender, was named the Ilana Kloss Playoff MVP even though Ottawa lost.

SOCCER

UPSET CITY!

In one of the soccer year's biggest upsets, English team Arsenal surprised Spanish club Barcelona to win the 2025 Women's Champions League. Amanda Ilestedt and Lina Hurtig danced with the trophy after their team's 1-0 victory gave Arsenal its first European championship since 2012. Barcelona missed out on its third straight title. There was lots more to the world of soccer in 2024–25. Put on your cleats and turn the page to recap all the action!

The Orlando Pride had a lot of reasons to celebrate in 2024. One was a league record for points.

NWSL 2024

The National Women's Soccer League continued to grow in both popularity and size during 2024, riding a big wave of interest in women's sports. In August, the players signed one of the best league players' contracts in the world. They'll make more money than ever before plus have a huge say in where they play. It was a big sign of the growth of women's soccer and women's sports overall.

During the 2024 season, the Orlando Pride rose way above the league, at one point going 24 games in a row without a loss (including part of 2023). They finished with a record 60 points, as well as 18 wins—the most in an NWSL season. They won their first Supporters' Shield as the team with the best regular-season record.

The Washington Spirit, a team that has rarely sniffed the heights of the standings, also won six of its first nine games. Their start was not a fluke. They finished with 56 points, their most ever, and tied the Pride for that league-record 18 wins.

Before the season, defending league champion Gotham FC aimed to become a superteam by adding four USWNT members: **Tierna Davidson**, **Crystal Dunn**, **Rose Lavelle**, and **Emily Sonnett**. Did it pay off? It did in the regular season, as they finished third with 56 points.

In their fourth season, the Kansas City Current finally got it all together. The team had never finished higher than fifth in a season since joining the league in 2020. But by June, they were in first place, with no losses in their first 15 games. KC finished fourth, its best result ever.

Meanwhile, two new teams made their NWSL debuts in 2024. Bay FC got 11 wins, setting a new first-season record, and made the playoffs. Utah managed only 7 wins in the season. Bay FC was also part of a milestone game in June. They played the Chicago Red Stars at Wrigley Field, home of MLB's Chicago Cubs. A crowd of 35,038 fans packed the old ballpark (which opened in 1914!) to set a new single-game NWSL attendance record.

The whole league took a break during the Summer Olympics, in which a record 56 NWSL players took part. Nineteen of the 22 players on the full US roster played in the Games. They brought home their fifth gold medal, the most ever!

While the Olympics went on, NWSL players kept the action hot back home with the Summer Cup. (See page 136.)

When everyone returned from Paris, the action heated up as Orlando and Washington tried to hold on to the top spots. Orlando beat Gotham 2-0 in a battle of top teams. Soon after, Gotham beat Utah to move into third place and clinch a playoff spot, joining Orlando, Kansas City, and Washington. A late-season win over Orlando showed that the defending champs were aiming for another title.

A highlight of the season was **Temwa Chawinga** setting a new single-season scoring record, smacking in 20 goals (the old record was 18). The Current forward from Malawi was in her first NWSL season. Success was not a surprise; she scored 84 goals in 84 games in a pro league in China and is the top scorer for her national team.

USWNT's Davidson joined Gotham in 2024.

NWSL News & Notes

THANKS, ALEX! One of the greatest American soccer players retired in 2024. **Alex Morgan** won two World Cups and an Olympic gold medal. She also played 10 years in the NWSL. Morgan's 123 goals for the US team are the fifth-most ever, and her 60 NWSL goals are fourth-most. She was also a leader off the field, calling for equal pay and rights for women in sports. Morgan left the field for the final time in the 13th minute of a San Diego Wave game. Why 13? That was her jersey number! (Bonus thanks to Portland's **Christine Sinclair**, a Canadian and the all-time leader in international goals. After 11 NWSL seasons—and 25 in pro soccer—she also retired.)

Alex and daughter, Charlie

SUMMER CUP 2024

The NWSL stopped regular-season play for six weeks because so many players were taking part in the Summer Olympics. But that still left lots of players looking for action! The NWSL x Liga MX Femenil Summer Cup included all 14 NWSL teams and six teams from Mexico's pro league in a mini-tournament. After group-stage games, four NWSL teams reached the semifinals. Liga MX teams won only three games against NWSL teams. An early second-half goal by **Delanie Sheehan** was all Gotham FC needed to beat Angel City FC 1-0. **Temwa Chawinga** got the KC Current off to a fantastic start with a second-minute goal, part of a 2-0 win over the NC Courage. In the championship game in October (with all the Olympians back!) the Current defeated Gotham FC 2-0 behind two goals by Chawinga.

Chawinga (right) led the way for KC.

Williams was a three-time league leader.

NEW NO. 1!

With a header in May against Chicago, **Lynn Williams** (now Biyendolo) scored her 79th goal in all NWSL competitions (regular season, playoffs, and cups). That makes her the league's No. 1 all-time in finding the back of the net. A powerful forward, Williams has played in the NWSL since 2016 and has helped her teams win three league titles. She scored her record-setting goal for Gotham FC and also has 21 goals for the USWNT. Williams ended the 2024 season with 84 total NWSL goals.

2024 NWSL AWARDS

MOST VALUABLE PLAYER
GOLDEN BOOT (TOP SCORER)
Temwa Chawinga
KC CURRENT

DEFENDER OF THE YEAR
Emily Sams
ORLANDO PRIDE

GOALKEEPER OF THE YEAR
Ann-Katrin Berger ▶▶▶
GOTHAM FC

ROOKIE OF THE YEAR
Croix Bethune
WASHINGTON SPIRIT

COACH OF THE YEAR
Seb Hines
ORLANDO PRIDE

NWSL Semifinals

Washington 1, Gotham 1

Washington wins in PKs, 3-0

The defending champs from New York nearly had a chance to repeat. They held on to a 1-0 lead thanks to a great header by **Esther**. But the Spirit had the home crowd on its side. They kept attacking and finally scored in the 93rd minute. **Hal Hershfelt** knocked in the tying goal on a corner kick. After a scoreless overtime came penalty kicks. Washington goalie **Aubrey Kingsbury** came up huge! She stopped not one, not two, but *three* Gotham kicks. The Spirit headed to its first NWSL Championship game.

Orlando 3, Kansas City 2

When you have the GOAT, you have a chance. Orlando had set a league record for points in the regular season but found themselves clinging to a 2-1 lead late in this game. Then Orlando's **Marta**, the amazing Brazilian some call the best women's soccer player ever, showed her magic. She got the ball just past the midfield line and raced to the goal. She dribbled past three Current players and the goalie to knock in what proved to be the game-winner in the 82nd minute. Check the video; it was an awesome goal!

Washington's players surround goalie Kingsbury after her awesome PK saves.

NWSL Championship

Banda's goal was all the Pride needed.

Pride 1, Spirit 0

Mother's Day is usually in May, but for Orlando star **Marta**, it came in late November. The Brazilian star led the Pride to its first NWSL Championship. It was also the first time that Marta's mother had ever seen her play in the NWSL!

Barbra Banda scored the game's only goal in the 37th minute. After getting a pass from **Angelina**, she carried the ball into the penalty area. She then cut back past a defender and whipped in a left-footed shot that got by Washington goalie **Aubrey Kingsbury**. That gave Banda a new NWSL single-playoffs record total of four goals. The Pride also tied an NWSL team scoring record with eight goals in the postseason.

Washington kept up the pressure after Banda's goal and outshot the Pride by a lot. But the Pride defense came up big to protect the shutout. After the game, Marta joyously held up the trophy, knowing her mom was watching from the stands!

"Hey, Mom, look what I won!"

"Messi" League Soccer

Of course, it's really Major League Soccer, but in 2024, superstar **Lionel Messi** was the biggest story . . . by far. He had joined Inter Miami in late 2023, so this was his first full season in MLS. Inter Miami got off to a great start, winning or tying 15 of their first 18 games. In the first seven games he played, Messi contributed to 16 goals, a new MLS record. Two of those came in a win over New England in front of 65,612 fans, a new Revolution record.

Everywhere Miami played, fans filled the stadium. There were often more Miami-pink shirts in the stands than shirts for the home team! In a win over the New York Red Bulls, Messi set an MLS record with 5 assists . . . in one half! By the end of April, he was leading the league in both goals and assists. Injuries cut him down to 19 games, but he still scored 20 goals, tying for second in the league. He also tied for third with 16 assists. All that led to Inter Miami having the best regular season in MLS history. Their 74 points and .765 winning percentage were the best ever.

Cincinnati and Columbus were hot on Miami's heels in the Eastern Conference. Columbus was hoping to repeat as MLS champs. In the Western Conference, the LA Galaxy had a rebound after several bad seasons. They had the top record after a third of the season. Helping the Galaxy were two European stars, **Marco Reus** (Germany) and **Olivier Giroud** (France). The Galaxy slipped a bit in May, and Minnesota and Real Salt Lake moved to the top ranks.

In July, LAFC scored a big 2-1 victory over the Galaxy in El Tráfico. That game was a sign of another big story in 2024: MLS TV ratings and attendance were up again. Some teams were selling out every game, and there was even talk of

Lionel Messi

The annual LA vs. LA "El Tráfico" packed the Rose Bowl once again.

needing new and bigger stadiums to handle the crowds. Several MLS games topped 60,000 fans, including El Tráfico at the Rose Bowl, which drew more than 70,000 people. Afterward, those two LA teams went down to the last game for the top spot in the West.

In July, 14-year-old **Cavan Sullivan** became the youngest player in MLS history when he played for the Philadelphia Union. Soon after, MLS took a break while the Olympics were played in Paris. Fifteen MLS players took part there, too!

In September, Messi returned from missing two months with an ankle injury. No problem—he got two goals and an assist to help Miami win and hold on to the league's best record. After winning the non-MLS US Open Cup, LAFC clinched a playoff spot by beating second-seeded Cincinnati 2-1 in late September. On the season's final Saturday, LAFC grabbed the top spot when the Galaxy gave up a stoppage-time goal to Houston. On that same day, Messi had a hat trick and an assist as Miami beat New England 6-2 to clinch their record-setting season.

After all that excitement, would the playoffs keep the action going? Let's find out!

2024 MLS PLAYOFF TEAMS

EASTERN CONFERENCE	POINTS	WESTERN CONFERENCE	POINTS
1. MIAMI	74	1. LAFC	64
2. COLUMBUS	66	2. LOS ANGELES	64
3. CINCINNATI	59	3. SALT LAKE	59
4. ORLANDO	52	4. SEATTLE	57
5. CHARLOTTE	51	5. HOUSTON	54
6. NEW YORK CITY	50	6. MINNESOTA	52
7. NEW YORK	47	7. COLORADO	50
8. MONTRÉAL	43	8. VANCOUVER	47
9. ATLANTA	40	9. PORTLAND	47

Reyes (No. 4) leaped through the Orlando defense to score for New York.

MLS Semifinals

EASTERN CONFERENCE

NY Red Bulls 1, Orlando City 0

There has been a New York Red Bulls team in MLS since the league's first season in 1994, but none of those teams have won a title. The Red Bulls hadn't even played in an MLS Cup since 2008! That second streak ended with this big win, thanks to a goal by **Andrés Reyes**. Ranked No. 7 in the regular season, the Red Bulls became the lowest-ranked team ever to battle to a spot in an MLS Cup. They had to beat the previous champs, Columbus, in an earlier round, too.

WESTERN CONFERENCE

LA Galaxy 1, Seattle Sounders 0

The Galaxy have won five MLS Cups, more than any other team. But their last one came way back in 2014. The last couple of seasons have been rough. They have not had a winning season since 2017, and in 2023 were 13th (out of 14) in their conference. But some new players, new team leaders, and loyal fans have helped them turn it around big-time. This year's squad tied team records with 69 goals and 19 wins. **Dejan Joveljić** wrote the latest chapter with his 86th-minute goal to beat the Sounders.

2024 MLS Cup

LA Galaxy 2, NY Red Bulls 1

The Galaxy added a sixth star to their jerseys, showing they have won more MLS Cups than any other team. Their latest came thanks to a defensive stand that lasted more than 75 minutes. **Joseph Paintsil** opened the scoring with a nice goal in the ninth minute. He took a perfect pass from **Gastón Brugman** and smacked it past the Red Bulls keeper. Less than five minutes later, **Dejan Joveljić** doubled the Galaxy's lead with a nifty toe-poke while being swarmed by defenders. New York got a goal back in the 28th minute after a goal-mouth scramble. Defender **Sean Nealis** trapped the ball with his chest and then volleyed in the goal.

MLS AWARDS

MOST VALUABLE PLAYER
LIONEL MESSI, Inter Miami

GOLDEN BOOT (TOP GOAL SCORER)
CHRISTIAN BENTEKE, DC United

DEFENDER OF THE YEAR
STEVEN MOREIRA, Columbus

GOALKEEPER OF THE YEAR
KRISTIJAN KAHLINA, Charlotte FC

NEWCOMER OF THE YEAR
GABRIEL PEC, LA Galaxy

YOUNG PLAYER OF THE YEAR
DIEGO LUNA, Real Salt Lake

Joveljić gave LA a game-winning goal.

From then on, the Red Bulls made attack after attack, but the Galaxy defense held them off. Both teams had chances to score again, but the 2-1 score held up for a dramatic finish. The Galaxy managed to win even after losing star midfielder **Riqui Puig** to an injury in the Western Conference final. The MLS Cup capped off a huge turnaround for the LA team. The Cup was back in LA, joining the five others the Galaxy has won, the most ever in MLS!

2025 Champions League

The UEFA Champions League (UCL) continues to be the second-best soccer event around. The World Cup is number one, of course, but we only see that every four years. We get a UCL every summer, and the 2025 competition was awesome. Here are some highlights of the early rounds. (For the first time, teams were split into "leagues" of nine teams with one game against each team in a group. The top eight in points moved on, the next 16 entered a playoff to advance, and the bottom 12 were eliminated.)

Englishman Kane made history for Munich.

League Stage

- Manchester City and Paris St.-Germain, two of the world's biggest clubs, just barely made it past the first round! Meanwhile, Liverpool finished on top of the standings. The team was on a roll in 2025, as it also won the Premier League (page 150).
- Bayern Munich set an all-time UCL record in a 9-2 win over Zagreb. Bayern's **Harry Kane** became the first player with three penalty-kick goals in a CL game. He also became the all-time UCL scoring leader among players from England.
- In the two teams' first meeting ever, French club Lille shocked huge favorite Real Madrid 1-0. Lille finished a surprising seventh in the group stage.
- Aston Villa got off to a surprise 3–0 start, including an upset of Bayern Munich and was eighth after the first round.
- Feyenoord shocked Manchester City, coming back from being down 3-0 to tie 3-3. It was the first time ever in the Champions League that a team blew a 3-0 lead in the final 15 minutes!

Yamal showed he's a future superstar.

Knockout Rounds

- The French team Brest was playing in its first-ever Champions League. After finishing a surprising 18th, they got swamped by Paris St.-Germain in the next round, losing 10-0 over the two-game contest.
- Real Madrid got a hat trick from **Kylian Mbappé** to send Manchester City, the defending champs, home from the tournament.
- Three Italian teams were upset in the first knockout round, with only Inter Milan making it to the final 16.
- Liverpool was knocked out in the round of 16 by PSG on penalty kicks.
- **Lamine Yamal** scored for Barcelona as they beat Benfica. Then just shy of 18 years old, he was the youngest player ever to both score and have an assist in a Champions League match!
- In the round of eight, Arsenal's **Declan Rice** scored two perfect free kicks to lead his team to a 3-0 win over Real Madrid.
- In a 2-0 win by Juventus over Manchester City, **Weston McKennie** had an assist on a goal by **Tim Weah**. It was the first time that a pair of US national team players teamed up to score in a UCL game!

It's going in! Rice (41) watches as his free kick curves toward the goal.

Champions League Semifinals

Inter 7, Barcelona 6

This was an instant classic. Two top teams went toe-to-toe and played a pair of memorable games. In the first game of the total-goals playoff, Inter Milan shocked Barcelona, the home team, with two goals in the first 21 minutes. Barça fought back, with young star **Lamine Yamal** curling in a left-footed strike and **Ferran Torres** tying the score. Milan went up again in the second half, but then **Raphinha**'s shot was so hard it bounced off Milan goalie **Yann Sommer** to make the final score 3-3. While that game was exciting, the return match was even better! This game was in Milan, and the home team led 2-0 early on. But as in game one, Barcelona bounced back in the second half, scoring twice, including the tying goal in the 60th minute. With just three minutes left in regular time, Raphinha scored to silence the home crowd and put Barcelona up 3-2. It wasn't over! In injury time, Milan's **Francesco Acerbi** scored an excellent one-touch goal at the near post to tie the score again at 3-3! On to 30 minutes of extra time. Both teams had chances early, but it was Milan that broke through. **Davide Frattesi** sent a left-footed shot into the far side of the net. Thanks in part to Sommer's incredible late saves, the Italian team held on for a fantastic 4-3 victory.

PSG 3, Arsenal 1

Compared to the other semifinal, this matchup wasn't nearly as exciting, unless you cheered for Paris St.-Germain. In the first game, **Ousmane Dembélé** scored in only the fourth minute . . . and that was it. The PSG defense did not allow Arsenal to score in the English team's home stadium. In Paris for the second game, PSG scored two goals in the first half and goalie **Gianluigi Donnarumma** had excellent saves, leading to a 2-1 win and a trip to the final.

Davide Frattesi

PSG captain Marquinhos hoists his team's first-ever Champions League trophy!

Champions League Final

Paris St.-Germain 5, Inter Milan 0

The Italian club Inter Milan took the pitch wearing gold uniforms. After the game, it was the French team from Paris who took home the gold . . . medals, that is. PSG finally won its first Champions League title by pounding Inter Milan. The score set a record for most goals in a Champions League final as well as biggest winning margin. **Achraf Hakimi**, a former Inter Player, put in the first goal for PSG in just the 12th minute after a perfect assist pass from **Désiré Doué**. Doué then doubled the score eight minutes later. His right-footed shot glanced off a defender's foot and into the net. At just 19, Doué became the youngest player ever with an assist and a goal in a Champions League final.

He became a double goal-scorer in the 63rd minute. A perfect pass from **Vitinha** left Doué alone against Inter goalie Yann Sommer, and the young Frenchman calmly buried the shot into the bottom corner. At 3-0, the game was basically over. PSG made their victory complete with goals from **Khvicha Kvaratskhelia** and **Senny Mayulu**.

Coach **Luis Enrique** had done what no coach in PSG history had done: bring home the European title. Several seasons after trying to win it all with megastars **Lionel Messi**, **Kylian Mbappé**, and **Neymar**, PSG got it done with teamwork and hard effort. Viva PSG!

2025 Women's Champions League

Sixteen of the top women's soccer teams in Europe earned spots in the 2025 Champions League. They were split into four groups of four teams, which played each other twice. The top two teams from each group moved into the playoff rounds. Here are some early-round highlights.

Aitana Bonmatí (left) led Barcelona.

- Only Lyon from France and Chelsea from England won all six of their matches. No surprise for Lyon, which has won this tournament a record eight times.
- Arsenal had to beat powerful Bayern Munich in the final group-stage game to win Group C.
- Arsenal and Lyon made the quarterfinals for the 16th time each, the all-time record.
- Turkish team Galatasaray had the toughest time, scoring only one goal and giving up 28 while losing all six matches.
- With Chelsea, Manchester City, and Arsenal all making it through, England was the first nation to have three teams make the final eight.
- Barcelona had an easy time in the quarterfinals, beating Wolfsburg from Germany by a combined score of 10-2!

Arsenal's players show just how much they enjoy being Champions League winners!

Semifinals

(Two-game totals shown)

Barcelona 8, Chelsea 2

Chelsea might be the best team in England, but it could not match Barcelona's firepower. The team from Spain won both matchups 4-1. **Cláudia Pina** scored twice in the first game and once in the second. It was Barcelona's sixth time in the championship game.

PIna and Putellas celebrate a Barça goal.

Arsenal 5, Lyon 3

In a bit of an upset, Arsenal came back with a big 4-1 win in the second game to earn a spot in the title game. Lyon had won the first matchup 2-1, but Arsenal got three goals in the first half of the second game and held off Lyon's attack to win.

Championship Game

Arsenal 1, Barcelona 0

For the last ten seasons, only two different teams have won the women's Champions League trophy: Barcelona and Lyon. After Arsenal sent Lyon home in the semifinals, could they repeat themselves in the final? Few gave them much chance against a Spanish team that had not lost in its last 24 games. Barcelona also featured two players who have each won the World Player of the Year award: **Aitana Bonmatí** and **Alexia Putellas**. But Arsenal's **Stina Blackstenius** scored after a pass from **Beth Mead** in the 74th minute for the game's only goal. One expert called it "one of the biggest upsets in Champions League history."

2024–25 Premier League

Salah was the EPL's top player for the second time.

Liverpool got off to a hot start in the 2024–25 season . . . and never cooled off. They opened up 12–1–1, making everyone else chase them. The Reds won their first Premier League championship since 2020. It was a return to the top for one of England's most famous teams, which had won 20 championships at the country's top level before this season. **Mohamed Salah** was the key man for the champs, leading the league with both 29 goals and 18 assists. His creative play, the speed of forward **Luis Díaz**, and the solid-wall defense of captain **Virgil van Dijk** made Liverpool very hard to beat. They clinched the title with four games left!

The late drama this season was not about who would be the champ, but about who would earn spots in the Champions League. The top five finishers in points would each get a spot. On the season's final day, three of those spots were still up for grabs among five teams. With Liverpool and number two Arsenal all set, Newcastle United, Manchester City, and Chelsea had to win to keep their spots in the big-money event. They all did, and Aston Villa and Nottingham Forest went home (almost) empty-handed.

McTominay's acrobatic goal helped Napoli earn a surprise Italian league title.

Other European Leagues

Spain (La Liga)

Spain is all about two teams: Barcelona and Real Madrid. Madrid was the defending champ, but in 2025, Barcelona returned to the top for the 28th time. They beat Madrid four times in league games or cup games, led by the amazing teenager **Lamine Yamal**. How good was he? After the season, he signed a new deal to possibly earn more than $40 million a season. He didn't turn 18 until July!

Germany (Bundesliga)

It was back to the top for Bayern Munich. The mighty team did not win it all in 2023–24, finishing third. But behind English striker **Harry Kane**'s 26 goals, the famous team got back the title for the 33rd time.

France (Ligue 1)

It was over early in France. Paris St.-Germain won its 13th French championship with six games left on the schedule. They lost only two games in the whole season!

Italy (Serie A)

Napoli needed to win its last game to earn the season championship . . . and they did. **Scott McTominay** whacked in an overhead kick for the game's first goal, and Napoli ended up winning 2-0. It was their fourth title and first since 2023.

Sjoeke Nusken, Mayra Ramirez, and Hannah Hampton of Chelsea celebrate their title.

2024–25 Women's Super League

How do you win a championship? Simple. Don't lose. That's what Chelsea did in the 2024–25 Women's Super League, played by 12 teams in England. Chelsea repeated as champs, but were even more special in 2024–25, winning 19 games and tying three while losing . . . none! It was actually six titles in a row now for Chelsea, one of the world's powerhouse teams. It was the second time they have gone undefeated for a season, too.

Chelsea clinched this season's title with two games left. **Lucy Bronze**, a star defender, headed in the game's only goal in a 1-0 win over Manchester United. That set off the celebrations that softened the sting of having lost in the Champions League the week before.

Agnes Beever-Jones led the way for Chelsea with nine goals, followed by **Guro Reiten**. For the whole WSL, Arsenal's **Mariona Caldentey** was the player of the year, while **Khadija Shaw** and **Alessia Russo** tied at 12 goals as the Golden Boot winners. But the most important trophy went home to Chelsea.

Caldentey (left) was the top player.

Other European Women's Leagues

SPAIN

As in the men's league, in Spain, it's all about Barcelona and Real Madrid. In 2024–25, Barcelona's women's team completed the double started by the men. The women won 28 of their 30 games on the season. **Ewa Pajor** had an awesome season with 25 goals and 9 assists.

Pajor was the top Spanish scorer.

FRANCE

Lyon won its 18th league title in France, beating Paris St.-Germain 3-0 in the final playoff game. Like Chelsea in England, Lyon didn't lose all season, winning 20 games and tying two. It was the fourth championship in a row for Lyon, which was led by defender **Wendie Renard** and top goal-scorer **Melchie Dumornay**, who banged in 16 scores.

Harder (center) celebrates with teammates.

GERMANY

As in Spain and France, Bayern Munich's women's team matched the men's as champion. The women lost only one game all season, finishing ahead of Wolfsburg. **Pernille Harder** from Norway led the way for the champs with 14 goals. She was also named player of the year for the league, while Bayern also won the German Cup tournament.

TOP OF THE BRICKYARD

Kyle Larson celebrates atop his car after winning the Brickyard 400 in Indianapolis. Why the bricks? The famous track was once covered with them. Today, only a finish-line strip remains. It was Larson's fourth win of the 2024 season.

NASCAR 2024

The 2024 NASCAR season was packed with great races, tight finishes, and even some off-track arguing! The Chase for the Cup Playoff was packed with excitement, and the final came down to the last seconds!

The 2024 Daytona 500 winner, **William Byron**, was star of the first half of the season. He won his second race at Circuit of the Americas in Texas, and he won his third at Martinsville Speedway. In April, **Chase Elliott**, a fan favorite, broke a 42-race losing streak. He earned a Playoff spot with a win at Texas Motor Speedway. At the mighty Talladega track in Alabama, a crash on the last lap let **Tyler Reddick** sneak through the wreckage for the win.

Chase Elliott was finally back on top in Texas.

At Dover Motor Speedway, **Denny Hamlin** squeaked ahead at the finish line, becoming the second driver to win three races. In Kansas, fans saw the closest finish in NASCAR history. **Kyle Larson** won by .0001 seconds over **Chris Buescher**. Race officials had to study photos and video to see who won.

How do you win a race that doesn't end? By being in first place when the rain comes! **Christopher Bell** won the Coca-Cola 600 (even though it was only the Coca-Cola 370 or so when a huge rainstorm ended it).

Rule number one when you get into a car: Make sure you have enough gas. **Ryan Blaney** forgot that rule (or forgot to look!), and it cost him a race. Blaney was leading with two laps left at the race in Madison, Illinois, when his car conked out. **Austin Cindric** swooped by to grab the win, his first since 2022. Blaney punched his ticket back to the Playoff with a win in the first NASCAR Cup race ever held at the Iowa Speedway.

Alex Bowman earned his spot in the Chase with a win on the road course in Chicago, Illinois. The course twisted through city streets beneath enormous skyscrapers! And on the famous track at the Indianapolis Motor Speedway, Larson won his fourth race of the year in the Brickyard 400.

Austin Dillon really wanted to make the Playoff. He got his chance in August in Richmond, Virginia, but he made a few people unhappy. On the last lap, Dillon smacked his car into the back of **Joey Logano**'s, which made Logano spin out. Two other cars crashed as a result, but Dillon sped through to win. It was not really against the rules, but other drivers said it was poor sportsmanship. Later, NASCAR ruled that the win did not give Dillon an automatic spot in the Chase Playoff.

Reddick moved into the top spot in the season standings with a win at Michigan International Speedway, his second checkered flag of 2024. In the last regular-season race, **Chase Briscoe** won his first race of 2024 and grabbed a surprise Playoff spot.

With the field of 16 drivers set, start your reading engines to find out how the Chase went in 2024!

2024 CHASE FOR THE CUP

ROUND OF 16

RACE 1 ATLANTA: In the Chase Playoff, if you win a race, you move to the next round. **Joey Logano** kicked things off with a win in Atlanta. He needed overtime to do it, getting some shoves from teammate **Ryan Blaney** to just beat **Daniel Suárez**.

RACE 2 WATKINS GLEN: This tough road course did not help any of the Playoff racers. None finished higher than sixth, so it was down to the next week to see who would move on. Non-Playoff driver **Chris Buescher** won the race, his first victory of the season.

RACE 3 BRISTOL: **Kyle Larson** zoomed into the next round with a win at this famous Tennessee track. Former champs **Brad Keselowski** and **Martin Truex Jr.** were among the drivers eliminated from the Chase.

ROUND OF 12

RACE 4 KANSAS: The remaining Chase for the Cup drivers nearly all stumbled as non-Playoff driver **Ross Chastain** won his first race of the season. **William Byron**'s second-place finish put him atop the Playoff standings through four races.

Yikes! This massive crash shook up the field at Talladega, but no one was hurt.

Reddick celebrated in Charlotte.

RACE 5 TALLADEGA: For the second week in a row, a non-Playoff driver won. In a wild race filled with crashes (one of them involved 27 cars!), **Ricky Stenhouse Jr.** won in overtime. Among Playoff drivers, Byron was best in third place. Many drivers looked to Charlotte as their final shot at the next round.

RACE 6 CHARLOTTE: Four drivers would finish this race knocked out of the Playoff. Larson made sure he wasn't one of them by winning his sixth race of the season. **Tyler Reddick** made a big charge from back in the pack to squeak into the next round of the Playoff, too. **Alex Bowman** made it but was then disqualified because his car did not weigh enough. Bowman's exit let Logano squeeze back into the final eight.

ROUND OF 8

RACE 7 LAS VEGAS: Logano wasted no time moving into the championship race with a victory. He was lucky to stay in after Charlotte to have this chance.

RACE 8 MIAMI: Reddick joined Logano in the "final four" with a last-lap pass to win. Reddick's team owner is NBA legend **Michael Jordan**, who knows a thing or two about winning!

RACE 9 MARTINSVILLE: After just missing out on a win in Miami, Blaney finished first in this last race before the finals. He joined Reddick, Logano, and Byron in the final four. Byron was actually tied with **Christopher Bell** for the last Playoff spot. But Byron was given that slot after a postrace penalty to Bell for an illegal move on the final lap.

Whew! A Martinsville win saved Blaney (No. 12)!

Championship Race

Logano sped under the checkered flag to win!

NASCAR racers are all teammates as well as drivers. Their team owners put two or three cars in each race. But once the green flag drops, it's nearly always every driver for himself. As the championship race in Phoenix roared to the last lap, a pair of Penske Racing teammates each had a shot at the title.

Defending champion **Ryan Blaney** led for most of the race, trying to win back-to-back titles. But after a late restart, teammate **Joey Logano** shot past. Over the final laps, Blaney crept closer and closer. With the crowd on their feet after watching a terrific final race, the cars were zooming to the finish line. Could Blaney catch Logano?

Not quite.

Logano won by only 0.33 seconds to capture his third NASCAR Cup. Blaney was second, barely ahead of the other final Cup contenders **William Byron** (third) and **Tyler Reddick** (sixth). Logano is one of ten drivers to have won a trio of season championships.

Joey Logano

Other NASCAR Champions

Allgaier flew the victory flag for the first time.

XFINITY

It was a long wait to hold up a trophy. **Justin Allgaier** has been a NASCAR racer for 14 seasons but had never won a series title. That streak ended in Phoenix when he sped to the Xfinity Series title in the championship race. It had been an up-and-down season for the veteran. He had finished in the bottom third in nine races. But he came through when it counted most and shed tears of joy in Victory Lane.

TRUCK SERIES

Meanwhile, another driver was off to a fast start. In only his third season as a full-time driver, **Ty Majeski** raced home with the Truck Series title, his first ever. He saved his best for last, having gone winless through the Playoff until the final event in Phoenix. He led 132 of the 150 laps and was pulling away from the pack at the checkered flag.

Majeski (No. 98) sped ahead of the field to win.

Formula 1 2024

Max Verstappen has dominated Formula 1, winning the championship from 2021 to 2023. His 2024 season, though, took a bit more effort. Other racers kept Verstappen out of first place for six races in a row, and a record seven different drivers won at least one race. Still, after another fast start, the Dutch driver won the season title for the fourth straight year.

Verstappen won the season's first two races. Then his engine quit during the race in Australia, opening up the event to everyone else. **Carlos Sainz** of Ferrari zoomed to the lead and stayed there for his first win since 2023. But then things settled back into the groove, with Verstappen winning the next two races.

It was left to other racers to try to pick up second places. **Lando Norris** was a surprise No. 2 in China in April. Norris then did even better in Miami, winning his first F1 race and breaking Verstappen's and Red Bull's winning streak. But things got back to "normal" the week after when Verstappen held off Norris to win in Italy.

In Monaco, perhaps F1's most famous race, **Charles Leclerc** made his lifelong dream come true. The driver was born and raised in the tiny European country, and he won the race there for the first time. He celebrated his first F1 win since 2022 with dozens of family and friends.

In the race in Montreal, Canada, Verstappen won for the third year in a row. Later, the Austrian race was a mess for the season's two top winners. Verstappen and Norris crashed into each other with just seven laps left. **George Russell** of Mercedes took advantage and zoomed through to win his first race since 2022.

Mercedes made it two wins in a row at the British Grand Prix. Seven-time world

Norris had his best season, finishing second overall.

Sparks flew as Verstappen roared to nine race wins. Left: He shows how many F1 titles he has!

champ **Lewis Hamilton** won for the record ninth time at his home track; it was his first race win since 2021. Hamilton got his second win of the summer in an unusual way. He finished second behind Mercedes teammate Russell in Belgium. But Russell's car came in underweight, which is against the rules. He was disqualified, and Hamilton was given first place.

Norris continued his excellent 2024 season with a win at the Dutch Grand Prix. He finished ahead of Verstappen by 22 seconds, disappointing fans in the Netherlands, who were cheering for their hometown hero. Verstappen remained in first place overall, but his lead was shrinking. It shrank even more after the Italian Grand Prix. Leclerc won his second race of the summer, and Norris finished third, inching closer to the top.

Another winner emerged in Baku. **Oscar Piastri** held off Leclerc to win his first race of 2024—only his second ever. The race for the top got even tighter after Norris won his second race of the season in Singapore. Things almost improved for Norris at the US Grand Prix in late October. At race's end, he was in third, but penalties for leaving the track cost him a place. Leclerc won the race, and Verstappen ended up in third, adding to his points lead.

Sainz swept to victory in Mexico City, and Norris picked up points on Verstappen. He was second, and the Dutch champ was sixth. But Verstappen showed the kind of champion he is at the Brazil race. After starting 17th in the rain, Verstappen roared to the lead and held on for his eighth victory of 2024.

At Las Vegas, Verstappen finished fifth, clinching the season title over runner-up Norris. Russell won the race, with Hamilton second, giving Mercedes a first-and-second finish. Verstappen won the big prize of the day, of course!

IndyCar 2024

For the second season in a row, **Álex Palou** used a hot start and a steady hand at the wheel to win the IndyCar season title. It took until the last race to clinch the spot, and he won by a seat belt. A seat belt? Read on!

As defending champ, Palou continued his hot streak to begin 2024, winning the season-opening $1 Million Challenge race in Palm Springs. Racers took part in a series of events that led to a 12-car sprint. Palou took the top prize.

In the first full-length race, in Florida, **Josef Newgarden** finished ahead of teammate **Scott McLaughlin** in third. However, several weeks later, IndyCar officials said that the two Penske Racing team drivers had broken rules about in-car technology. Newgarden and McLaughlin were disqualified. That made **Pato O'Ward** the winner a long time after he climbed out of his car! It was a black mark for Penske, but they bounced back quickly. In the race after the news of the DQ came out, McLaughlin and **Will Power** finished first and second in Alabama. Steady work by **Colton Herta** had him in first place by late April, even though he had not won a race.

Herta's lead did not last long. Defending champ Palou steadily moved up the standings. On the road course in Indianapolis, he cruised to victory to take over the points lead, too.

Newgarden bounced back from the rule-breaking by winning his second Indy 500 in a row. The famous race came down to a last-lap duel. With two turns to go, the American zoomed past O'Ward for the checkered flag. Newgarden was the first back-to-back Indy winner since 2002.

At Road America in Wisconsin, the 2022 champion, Power, won his first race since that title-winning season. He also moved into first place in the 2024 standings—could he race to another crown?

Chadwick made history in the lower-division Indy NXT series.

Palou became the first back-to-back IndyCar champ since 2011.

The Indy NXT series is like the minor leagues of IndyCar. Racers there are aiming to get a chance at the "big" cars. In June, **Jamie Chadwick** became the first woman to win an Indy NXT race on a road course when she captured the Wisconsin event before Power's win. Only a few women have raced IndyCar; will Chadwick be next?

Meanwhile, in IndyCar, Herta had a big weekend in Toronto. At each IndyCar race, drivers take part in practice runs, qualifying laps, and the race itself. For the first time in the sport's history, Herta had the best times in every part of the event. It was Herta's first win of the season, too!

Newgarden likes the annual race in Illinois. He won for the fifth time on that circuit for his second victory of 2024. In Portland, the race for the top spot got tighter when Power won his third race of the season, trying to inch up on Palou in the points chase.

The second-to-last race of the season was a wild one. Held in Milwaukee, it included nearly 700 passes of one car by another, the most in 2024. There was also a three-car accident, a start that had to be done over, and defending champ Palou sitting in a car that would not run! Palou did eventually get the car going but finished 29 laps behind winner McLaughlin.

Heading into the final race of the season, Palou was in first place, but by only 33 points over Power. At Nashville, Power had a shot at overtaking the leader, but a broken seat belt kept him in the pits for far too long. Palou finished 11th in the race, but Power was way back in 24th, giving Palou enough points to make him a back-to-back champion.

Final IndyCar 2024 Top Five

PLACE/DRIVER	POINTS
1. **Álex PALOU** (RIGHT)	**544**
2. **Colton HERTA**	**513**
3. **Scott MCLAUGHLIN**	**505**
4. **Will POWER**	**498**
5. **Pato O'WARD**	**460**

GOLF

AMERICAN MADE
Nelly Korda celebrates after sinking a putt in the United States' victory in the Solheim Cup late in the 2024 golf season. (See page 166.) After dominating the field in 2024, Korda opened the 2025 season as the world's No. 1–ranked women's player.

Wrapping Up 2024

In 2024, the golf world boasted not one but two of the greatest seasons in its history: Nelly Korda on the women's side and Scottie Scheffler on the men's.

A Dominant Year

Early in the 2024 golf season, American **Nelly Korda** was unbeatable. From January through April, she won five straight times. That tied the LPGA record shared by Hall of Famers **Nancy Lopez** (1978) and **Annika Sorenstam** (2004–05). But Korda wasn't done. She added two more wins by season's end to finish with seven titles in all. It was the most by an LPGA Tour player since 2011, and the most by an American woman since 1990! The Florida-born star added three other top-10 finishes in her amazing year and was named the LPGA Player of the Year.

Scheffler shows off his FedEx Cup.

Matching Sevens

Nelly Korda's seven wins were matched by fellow American **Scottie Scheffler** on the PGA Tour. The No. 1–ranked Scheffler became the first men's player to win seven times in one season on the PGA Tour since **Tiger Woods** in 2007. Scheffler's many highlights included his second career win at the Masters and his second win in a row at the Players Championship. No one had ever won that tournament in back-to-back seasons. He also won an Olympic gold medal. Scheffler capped his remarkable year by winning the FedEx Cup—and the $25 million prize that went with it—for the first time.

TEAM OF LEGENDS **Nelly Korda** and WNBA star **Caitlin Clark** (right) paired up in a pro-am event called the Annika, hosted by LPGA legend **Annika Sorenstam** in Florida. After playing her first nine holes with Korda, Clark played the next nine alongside Sorenstam. Clark learned what just about everyone who has ever picked up a golf club already knows. "Golf is hard," she said.

U-S-A! U-S-A!

International team competitions are highlights of the golf calendar. In 2024, the United States team won both the Solheim Cup (women) and the Presidents Cup (men).

US team members Sarah Schmelzel and Korda

Solheim Cup

For the first time since 2017, the United States won the Solheim Cup. The team of American women defeated Europe 15.5-12.5 in Virginia in September. The US squad jumped to a 3-1 lead in the Day 1 morning session, and held a commanding 6-2 advantage after the afternoon matches. It was 10-6 after Day 2. In Day 3's 12 single matches, the Europeans couldn't pull off a comeback.

American **Rose Zhang** became just the eighth player in Solheim Cup history to win all four of her matches in the competition. Virginia native **Lauren Coughlin** went 3–0–1 in her matches, and world No. 1 **Nelly Korda** was 3–1.

Collin Morikawa

Presidents Cup

Every two years, this event pits golfers from the United States against golfers from outside of Europe. In the fall of 2024, in Montreal, Canada, the Americans beat the International team 18.5-11.5 to win the competition for the tenth time in a row.

The United States looked like it would run away with the event when they swept the five matches on opening day. But the International team countered by sweeping the five matches the next day to even the score. Then on Day 3, the Americans retook control by winning six out of the eight matches. That was too big of a hurdle for the Europeans to overcome in singles on the final day. **Patrick Cantlay**, **Collin Morikawa**, and **Xander Schauffele** each won four of their five Cup matches.

2025 News and Notes

Indoor pro golf has arrived with TGL.

GOLF TECH

Tomorrow's Golf League (TGL) teed up for the first time in January 2025. TGL was founded by pro stars **Rory McIlroy** and **Tiger Woods**. TGL combines "top technology with teams of top players from the PGA Tour." Basically, it's golf played on a simulator—until players reach the green. Then a hydraulic-powered green changes shape to create a different putting surface for each hole. Six teams competed at a custom-built studio in Florida in the league's first season. The Atlanta Drive Golf Club, won the championship.

SHORT WAIT

It didn't take long for **Ingrid Lindblad** to make her mark on the LPGA Tour. The native of Sweden turned pro in 2025. And in just her third time out, she won the JM Eagle LA Championship in Los Angeles in April. Watch for more from the former world No. 1 amateur player.

HAPPY ST. PATRICK'S DAY!

McIlroy, who was born and raised in Holywood, County Down in Northern Ireland, won the 2025 Players Championship in a Monday playoff on March 17. That's St. Patrick's Day, the Christian feast day celebrating the patron saint of Ireland. In the playoff that day, McIlroy got a little luck of the Irish. His opponent, **J.J. Spaun**, saw his tee shot blown by the wind into the water. McIlroy danced home for the win.

Here Comes the Son

Tiger Woods is probably the greatest golfer of all time. But there's a new Woods coming: his son, **Charlie**. In May 2025, 16-year-old Charlie won his first American Junior Golf Association title. Keep an eye on this rising star!

Men's 2025 Majors

The major championships in men's golf have become even more important in recent years. That's because they are the only events (along with the Players Championship) at which the very best players from the PGA Tour, LIV Golf, and DP World Tour are on the same course at the same time.

Career Slam

It wasn't easy, but **Rory McIlroy** overcame a roller-coaster final round to win the 2025 Masters Tournament and complete the career Grand Slam. That means winning all four men's major championships. The Northern Ireland golfer had already won the US Open, British Open, and the PGA Championship (twice).

After four late bogies made his lead disappear, McIlroy was in a playoff with **Justin Rose**. McIlroy landed a perfect approach shot to win the hole and earn the famous green jacket. McIlroy joined these six other great "career Slam" winners: **Ben Hogan**, **Jack Nicklaus**, **Gary Player**, **Gene Sarazen**, and **Tiger Woods**.

Rory McIlroy

MEN'S 2025 MAJOR CHAMPIONS	
MASTERS	Rory McIlroy
PGA CHAMPIONSHIP	Scottie Scheffler
US OPEN	J.J. Spaun
BRITISH OPEN	Scottie Scheffler

Mile Run

The final three long, tricky holes at the Quail Hollow Club in North Carolina make up a long and brutal stretch called "the Green Mile." But they were no problem for **Scottie Scheffler**. The No. 1–ranked golfer tamed the "Mile" and wound up winning the 2025 PGA Championship by five strokes. His third-round 65 put him in control. It was the 28-year-old's 15th win on the PGA Tour, and his third major title.

The One and Only

In 2025, only one player finished under par at the US Open. That one player was **J.J. Spaun**, whose one-under score won! He had to overcome a string of late bogies that left him in a tie for first. But he birdied the 17th. On the 18th, he stunned the crowd and himself by burying a 64-foot putt to win! "I was just in shock, disbelief that it went in," Spaun said afterward. "It was a storybook, fairy-tale ending."

Women's 2025 Majors

The women's major championship season always starts off with a splash: The winner of the Chevron Championship at the Woodlands, Texas, traditionally takes a leap into the pond beside the 18th green. In 2025, that honor went to Japan's Mao Saigo—although it got a little scary for her!

Saigo (center) took a winning dip.

WOMEN'S 2025 MAJOR CHAMPIONS	
CHEVRON CHAMPIONSHIP	Mao Saigo
US WOMEN'S OPEN	Maja Stark
WOMEN'S PGA CHAMPIONSHIP	Minjee Lee
AMUNDI EVIAN CHAMPIONSHIP	Grace Kim
WOMEN'S BRITISH OPEN	Miyu Yamashita

"I'm not really a good swimmer. When I went inside, it was deep, and at first I thought I was going to drown." – MAO SAIGO

Last Woman Standing

At the Chevron Championship, **Mao Saigo** of Japan won for the first time on the LPGA Tour. She had to survive a wild series of events. Thailand's **Ariya Jutanugarn** arrived at the par-five 18th hole on Sunday in the lead. She just needed par to win. But she whiffed a chip shot when her club got stuck in the heavy rough near the green. That led to a bogey, dropping her into a tie with **Hyo Joo Kim** for the lead. Then Saigo, **Ruoning Yin**, and **Lindy Duncan** all made dramatic birdie putts. It was a five-golfer tie! In the sudden-death playoff, Yin reached the green in two, but she three-putted for par. Duncan, Jutanugarn, and Kim also parred. Only Saigo was able to make birdie. She hit a perfect approach shot to three feet, then made the putt to win.

How Swede It Is!

Sweden's **Maja Stark** outlasted No. 1–ranked **Nelly Korda** of the United States and **Rio Takeda** by two strokes each to win the 2025 US Women's Open. Stark entered the final round just one stroke clear of Spain's **Julia Lopez Ramirez**. But while Lopez Ramirez struggled to a final-round 79, Stark carded an even-par 72 and never gave up her lead. Stark became only the third player from Sweden to win the US Women's Open. The others are LPGA legends **Annika Sorenstam** (three times) and **Liselotte Neumann**.

TENNIS

FABULOUS IN FRANCE

American Coco Gauff continued a strong run through the tennis world by capturing her first French Open title—and second Grand Slam championship—with a win over world No. 1 Aryna Sabalenka. The match was played on the red-clay courts of Paris. *(See page 172.)*

2024 Tour Champs

The ATP (men's) and WTA (women's) tennis tours crown their season champion with an end-of-year tournament featuring the top eight players. After group play, the two players with the best records in each group advance to semifinal matches followed by the championship match.

Sinner won his first world title . . . at home!

"It's amazing. It's my first title in Italy and it means so much to me. It's something very special." – JANNIK SINNER

ATP Finals

Jannik Sinner won the ATP Finals when he beat American **Taylor Fritz** in straight sets in the championship match in Italy. Sinner, born in a village in northern Italy, became the first Italian to win the ATP Finals in the event's 55-year history. He also won the first ATP Finals tournament in 23 years that didn't include one of the Big Three: **Novak Djokovic**, **Rafael Nadal**, or **Roger Federer**.

The top-ranked player in the world, Sinner didn't lose a set while winning his five matches in the tournament—no player had done that in the ATP Finals in 38 years. And even though the score in the title match was close (6–4, 6–4), Sinner's victory never seemed in doubt. He won points on 83 percent of his first serves and needed only 85 minutes to close out the win.

WTA Finals

In 2024, **Coco Gauff** became the ninth different winner in the last nine WTA Finals (not including 2020, canceled due to COVID). She defeated China's **Zheng Qinwen** 3–6, 6–4, 7–6 in the final at Riyadh, Saudi Arabia. The 20-year-old American reached the final the hard way, beating world No. 2 **Iga Świątek** of Poland in the group stage, then knocking out top-ranked **Aryna Sabalenka** of Belarus in the semifinals. In a grueling final against Zheng, Gauff overcame a first-set loss and a 5–3 deficit in the third set.

The Atlanta-born Gauff was the first American woman to win the WTA Finals since **Serena Williams** in 2014.

Women's 2025 Grand Slams

With so many great players in women's tennis today, someone new seems to step up at every Grand Slam. When Coco Gauff won the French Open in 2025, she became the fifth different woman to win a major title in the last five events.

WOMEN'S 2025 GRAND SLAMS	
AUSTRALIAN OPEN	**Madison Keys**
FRENCH OPEN	**Coco Gauff**
WIMBLEDON	**Iga Świątek**
US OPEN	______________

WORTH THE WAIT

Madison Keys was seeded just No. 19 in the women's draw at the 2025 Australian Open. But in the end, the American was No. 1. Keys won the first Grand Slam title of her career by defeating the two-time defending champ **Aryna Sabalenka**, the top-ranked women's player in the world.

Keys had been just 19 years old and an emerging star when she reached the semifinals of the 2015 Australian Open. It seemed major titles would soon come her way. But it turned out her first Grand Slam title was still a decade away. She broke through in 2025, defeating four top-10 seeds while winning in Australia. "I finally got to the point where I was proud of myself and proud of my career, with or without a Grand Slam," Keys said afterward. Letting go like that "gave me the ability to actually go out and play some really good tennis to win a Grand Slam."

Keys with her shiny Aussie trophy

AN AMERICAN IN PARIS

Coco Gauff, the No. 2 player in the world, rallied to beat Sabalenka in three sets to win the French Open. It was the second career Grand Slam title for Gauff, who became the first American French Open champion since **Serena Williams** in 2015.

Gauff had reached the final by blasting local favorite **Lois Boisson** of France 6–1, 6–2 in the semifinals. But she had to work hard against Sabalenka. "I think the first [Grand Slam] was more emotional, but I think this one was just harder," Gauff said.

Men's 2025 Grand Slams

Who's your pick as the best player in men's tennis today? Jannik Sinner or Carlos Alcaraz? The two entered the summer of 2025 ranked one-two in the world and had a combined six consecutive Grand Slam titles. They played a French Open final in 2025 that will be talked about for a long time.

OUT OF THIS WORLD

Jannik Sinner is far away from **Novak Djokovic**'s record of 24 men's Grand Slam singles titles. But after losing to Sinner in the 2025 Australian Open final, **Alexander Zverev** said, "He's very, very similar to Novak when he was at his best." That's pretty high praise, but Sinner has earned it. He lost only two sets during his seven matches in Australia.

Sinner's victory marked his second Australian Open title in a row, and his third Grand Slam win in all. He also won the 2024 US Open. Sinner won't threaten Djokovic's career Grand Slam record anytime soon, but there was little doubt the No. 1–ranked Sinner was playing out of this world early in 2025. "He's in a different universe right now," Zverev added.

MEN'S 2025 GRAND SLAMS

AUSTRALIAN OPEN	**Jannik Sinner**
FRENCH OPEN	**Carlos Alcaraz**
WIMBLEDON	**Jannik Sinner**
US OPEN	________________

Alcaraz was magnifique in Paris.

THE FUTURE IS NOW

If it wasn't clear enough already, Sinner and Alcaraz cemented their place atop the men's tennis world with an epic final match at the 2025 French Open. Alcaraz came from behind for a five-set victory. It was the Spaniard's fifth career Grand Slam win and second in France.

After dropping the first two sets, Alcaraz won the third but fell behind 5–3 in the fourth and faced three match points. He fought them all off and went on to win the set, as well as a fifth-set tiebreaker. The final score was 4–6, 6–7, 6–4, 7–6, 7–6. It took five hours and 29 minutes—the second-longest Grand Slam final in history—to complete the back-and-forth struggle.

Tennis Notes 2025

Adios and gracias, Rafael!

One Hundred Times Two

Serbia's **Novak Djokovic** joined a new club after winning the Geneva Open in May 2025. He became just the third men's player in the Open Era (since 1968) with 100 career tournament wins. The others are **Jimmy Connors** (109) and **Roger Federer** (103). Djokovic later became just the second player to win 100 matches at the French Open.

When Work Is Play

France's **Gael Monfils** defeated Belgium's **Zizou Bergs** to win the ATP Tour stop in New Zealand 2025. At 38, Monfils became the oldest player ever to win an ATP title. It was the 13th tournament win of his long career. "I love tennis," Monfils said after his historic victory. "When you love something, it's easier to keep pushing."

Rafa Retires

After the 2024 Davis Cup, Spain's **Rafael Nadal** officially retired from tennis. "It is obviously a difficult decision and one that has taken me some time to make," he said. "But in this life, everything has a beginning and an end." The legendary 38-year-old closed his career with 92 singles titles, fifth-most among all men's players in the Open Era, including 22 Grand Slam singles titles.

Pickleball Slam

Pickleball is one of the fastest-growing sports in the United States. It's even

Smaller paddle, still big game for Graf

Li swings while Wang waits to help.

attracting big-time tennis stars. At the Pickleball Slam, husband-and-wife **Andre Agassi** (8 Grand Slam wins) and **Steffi Graf** (22) played US Open winner **Andy Roddick** and pro pickleballer **Eugenie Bouchard**. It was for big money and got a good TV audience. Agassi and Graf ended up on top; no word on whether they celebrated by eating pickles.

China Rising

China's first Grand Slam title in wheelchair tennis came in doubles at the 2025 Australian Open. **Wang Ziying** and **Li Xiaohui** teamed to beat **Zhu Zhenzhen** (also of China) and **Manami Tanaka** (of Japan) 6–2, 6–3 in the championship match.

That continued a strong stretch for Chinese players. At the 2024 Australian Open, **Zheng Qinwen** became the second player from China to reach a Grand Slam final in the main division. That same summer, Zheng went on to win her country's first Olympic gold medal in women's singles.

Tennis Hall of Fame

Maria Sharapova and brothers **Bob** and **Mike Bryan** were inducted into the International Tennis Hall of Fame in Newport, Rhode Island, in the summer of 2025.

Sharapova won 36 singles titles, including five Grand Slams and one WTA Tour Final (2004), in her pro career from 2001 to 2020. She is one of only 10 women to win each of the four Grand Slam events at least once. In 2005, her booming serve and strong backhand helped her become the first Russian woman to reach No. 1 in the world.

The California-born Bryan brothers formed the most successful doubles team in ATP history. They won 16 Grand Slam doubles titles, including six at the Australian Open and five at the US Open. Starting in 2003, they were No. 1 in the world rankings; they would be there for a record 438 weeks in their careers. In all, they won 119 doubles titles, plus an Olympic gold medal (2012), and they helped the US team win the Davis Cup in 2007.

Bob (left) and Mike . . . we think.

SHE'S NO. 1!
In 2025, Alysa Liu became the 14th American woman to be the world champ. She was part of a successful World Figure Skating Championships for American athletes.

Winter Sports

Shiffrin's skis say it all: 100 Ws!

FIGURE SKATING

Alysa Liu got off to a fast start in figure skating. In 2019, at 13, she was the youngest person ever to win the US championship. But she retired three years later, burned out at 16. In 2024, she decided to come back to the ice. It turned out to be a good move! At the 2025 World Championships, Liu took the gold medal. She was the first US skater since 2006 to win it all. In the final free skate, she landed seven triple jumps and won by nearly five points (that's a lot in figure skating!).

She was not the only big US story. Americans **Isabeau Levito** (fourth) and **Amber Glenn** (fifth) made it the best US showing since 2001 at the Worlds. **Ilia Malinin** made it a golden sweep by winning the men's singles as well. It was his second world title in a row. **Madison Chock** and **Evan Bates** won the ice dance gold for the US as well. **Riku Miura** and **Ryuichi Kihara** of Japan were the pairs champions.

WORLD CUP SKIING

Two skiers returned to the top of World Cup standings in 2024–25. Austria's **Marco Odermatt** won his fourth world title. **Federica Brignone** of Italy won her second. Odermatt dominated the rankings, finishing atop the downhill, giant slalom, and super G standings, too. Brignone also won the downhill and giant slalom championships.

American **Mikaela Shiffrin** battled injuries but still finished fourth. She won three slalom events, adding to her all-time world-record total of 101 race wins. She has also earned five world all-around titles. Another American superstar, **Lindsey Vonn**, made a comeback to the slopes. She used to hold the all-time women's World Cup wins record with 82, but retired six years ago. In 2024, at the age of 40, she decided to try again and took part in a dozen races. Her silver medal in a super-G race in Idaho made her the oldest World Cup medal winner ever!

THE BEST EVER **Francesco Friedrich of Germany earned his 100th win as the driver of a bobsled. He has won in two-man and four-man events and also has four Olympic gold medals. No one else is even close to his amazing career record. He has won 32 World Cup or World Championship overall titles, including team and individual wins.**

Chloe Kim continued her amazing streak in the halfpipe, earning another gold.

Winter X Games

Traditional skiers and skaters had their World Championships, but there was another winter sports competition that showed off some amazing talents! As always, the Winter X Games were packed with high-flying thrills and record-setting performances. There were new tricks, new champs, and a slightly new format. (For the first time, top-scoring athletes moved into a final playoff for the medals.) Some of the gold medalists were familiar names.

Lots and Lots of Gold

Alex Hall won Ski Knuckle Huck for his 12th career X Games medal. In snowboarding, **Anna Gasser** of Austria became the first woman to win four Big Air gold medals. And America's **Chloe Kim** continued her dominance of the halfpipe. She won her eighth gold, the most ever in the event by a woman in the X Games.

Stevenson soared into a gold medal!

American Heroes

While the X Games is a very international event,

athletes from the US took advantage of "home snow" to capture medals. **Rell Harwood** won the women's ski Knuckle Huck event, while Hall won the men's. **Colby Stevenson** earned gold in ski Street Style (and teammate **Tucker FitzSimons** won silver!). **Red Gerard** added to a long list of successes at the X Games with a win in snowboard Slopestyle. **Iris Pham** won snowboard Street Style. **Nick Goepper** won the ski SuperPipe event.

Did you see that? James hit a new trick.

Rookie Winners

A trio of rookies won their first golds on the event's second day: **Luca Harrington** of New Zealand (men's ski Slopestyle), **Flora Tabanelli** of Italy (women's ski Big Air), and **Wang Ziyang** of China (men's snowboard Knuckle Huck).

Hiroto Ogiwara

New Tricks

As for new tricks, fans cheered when **Scotty James** nailed the first-ever triple cork 1440 in snowboard SuperPipe. **Zoi Sadowski-Synnott** matched James' trick, but she did it in Slopestyle to win her first gold.

To win snowboard Big Air, **Hiroto Ogiwara** of Japan had to do a trick no one had ever done—a backside 2340. That means he zoomed into the air and spun six and a half times before landing!

"I am the first in the world to do that. I've never been as happy as this," Ogiwara told the media after. "It was really the greatest moment. It felt as if I used every ounce of energy I had."

To cap off a wild weekend, Tabanelli threw down a 2340 in ski Big Air!

NCAA Champions

Along with football, basketball, softball, and baseball (covered in other sections in this book), the NCAA has lots of other sports champs. Here are the best from 2024-25.

A tired but happy Northwestern cross-country team.

MEN

CROSS-COUNTRY
BYU

FENCING*
Notre Dame

GOLF
Oklahoma State

GYMNASTICS
Michigan

ICE HOCKEY
Western Michigan

INDOOR TRACK & FIELD
USC

LACROSSE
Cornell

OUTDOOR TRACK & FIELD
USC/ Texas A&M

RIFLE*
West Virginia

SKIING*
Utah

SOCCER
Vermont

SWIMMING & DIVING
Texas

TENNIS
Wake Forest

VOLLEYBALL
Long Beach State

*In these sports, men and women compete on the same teams.

WATER POLO
UCLA

WRESTLING
Penn State

WOMEN

BEACH VOLLEYBALL
TCU

BOWLING
Youngstown State

CROSS-COUNTRY
BYU

FIELD HOCKEY
Northwestern

GYMNASTICS
Oklahoma

ICE HOCKEY
Wisconsin

GOLF
Northwestern

INDOOR TRACK & FIELD
Oregon

LACROSSE
North Carolina

OUTDOOR TRACK & FIELD
Georgia

ROWING
Stanford

SOCCER
North Carolina

SWIMMING & DIVING
Virginia

TENNIS
Georgia

VOLLEYBALL
Penn State

WATER POLO
Stanford

Stanford celebrates another water polo national title.

Alvarado celebrates as he and Sovereignty cross the line at the Belmont Stakes.

2025 Triple Crown

Two horses dominated the three Triple Crown races. However, because one of the pair did not run in the second race in the series, racing fans did not enjoy a Triple Crown winner in 2025. Here's what happened in the three big races.

Kentucky Derby: **Journalism** came in as the favorite to win this famous race, which was first held back in 1875. And Journalism led early in the race. Meanwhile, **Sovereignty** (SAHV-rin-tee) was back in the pack until the final turn. Then jockey **Junior Alvarado** made his move. He urged Sovereignty to speed up. In the final straight, Sovereignty sprinted past Journalism to win the Derby.

Preakness Stakes: The owners and trainer of the Derby winner decided not to race Sovereignty in this event in Maryland. That left Journalism as the favorite and the horse came through with a big victory. Jockey **Umberto Rispoli** guided his mount to a late breakaway from the pack to win the second leg of the Triple Crown.

Belmont Stakes: As in Kentucky, this was a two-horse race at the end. And it ended the same way, with Sovereignty sprinting past Journalism at the end to win. The Belmont champ became the third horse since 2005 to win two races in the Triple Crown. Fans were left wondering whether Sovereignty could have won all three!

Premier Lacrosse League

When you have an MVP playing goalie, you have to feel good about your chances. For the second season in a row, **Brett Dobson** of the Utah Archers was named the top player of the PLL championship game. He had 17 saves to lead his team to a 12-8 win over the Maryland Whipsnakes.

It wasn't all Dobson, of course. In fact, he let in three goals to allow Maryland to get out to an early lead. But he and the defense buckled down while the Archers' offense went to work. **Mac O'Keefe** led the way with three goals, while **Matt Moore** and **Tre Leclaire** added two each.

O'Keefe (left) heads for the goal.

Ultimate Frisbee

Ultimate pros leap for the flying disc!

Ultimate Frisbee started in the 1960s as a way to add a bit of competition to flipping around a spinning disc. It became a popular sport at many colleges. It's a combination of frisbee throwing and catching, football, and a bit of gymnastics—some of the athletes make amazing, diving catches! Since 2012, it has become a pro sport, too. The Ultimate Frisbee Association (UFA) has 24 teams. They play a 12-game late-summer schedule; there's even a team in Montreal. The 2024 champion was the Minnesota Wind Chill. Check out the league online for 2025 championship results.

Beach Volleyball

On sand courts around the world throughout 2024, the best beach volleyball teams battled for top honors. They piled up points to earn a spot in the Finals, which were held in Qatar. The American team of **Molly Shaw** and **Toni Rodriguez** captured the championship for women, ahead of **Noa Sonneville** and **Brecht Piersma** of the Netherlands. In the men's event, **Anders Mol** and **Christian Sørum** of Sweden came out on top, beating Germany's **Paul Henning** and **Lui Wüst**.

Great defense like this helped Shaw win it all.

Major League Cricket

Bowled! A batter is out in an MLC match.

Cricket is a huge sport in many countries around the world. Many people from India, Pakistan, South Africa, England, and other places now can follow their favorite sport in the United States. Major League Cricket (MLC) has six teams from coast to coast. Top Americans are joined by stars from around the world. MLC teams played in Texas, Florida, and in the Oakland Coliseum, the former home of MLB's Athletics. The 2025 champion was MI New York.

Weird Sports!

So many sports, not enough pages! There are dozens and dozens of amazing sports that we could not squeeze into the Year in Sports. But let's fill you in on three very interesting competitions.

TEQBALL

(Below) This is what you get when you combine table tennis, foot tennis, and soccer. Players send a ball back and forth over a curved table using everything but their arms and hands. It calls for some serious gymnastic moves, too!

CANAL JUMPING

(Above) Only in the Netherlands, but they call it *fierljeppen*! Players in this odd sport sprint and then leap onto a pole sticking out of the water of a canal. They have to climb the pole while it falls to the opposite bank. If they don't climb fast enough . . . splash!

UNDERWATER HOCKEY

(Right) Everybody into the pool to play . . . hockey? Don't you need ice? Not in this version of the game. Teams of six move a weighed puck around the bottom of a pool. Swimmers have to hold their breath while playing. They wear masks and snorkels as well as a padded glove that holds a short stick. Only the referee stays underwater the whole time! Australia and New Zealand have dominated world competitions.

CHAMPIONS!

NFL

GAME	SEASON	RESULT
LIX	2024	**Philadelphia** 40, **Kansas City** 22
LVIII	2023	**Kansas City** 25, **San Francisco** 22
LVII	2022	**Kansas City** 38, **Philadelphia** 35
LVI	2021	**L.A. Rams** 23, **Cincinnati** 20
LV	2020	**Tampa Bay** 31, **Kansas City** 9
LIV	2019	**Kansas City** 31, **San Francisco** 20
LIII	2018	**New England** 13, **L.A. Rams** 3
LII	2017	**Philadelphia** 41, **New England** 33
LI	2016	**New England** 34, **Atlanta** 28
50	2015	**Denver** 24, **Carolina** 10
XLIX	2014	**New England** 28, **Seattle** 24

Luke Sawyer with Ohio State's big trophy

NFL MOST VALUABLE PLAYER

2024	**Josh ALLEN**, Buffalo
2023	**Lamar JACKSON**, Baltimore
2022	**Patrick MAHOMES**, Kansas City
2021	**Aaron RODGERS**, Green Bay
2020	**Aaron RODGERS**, Green Bay
2019	**Lamar JACKSON**, Baltimore
2018	**Patrick MAHOMES**, Kansas City
2017	**Tom BRADY**, New England
2016	**Matt RYAN**, Atlanta
2015	**Cam NEWTON**, Carolina

COLLEGE FOOTBALL

2024 **OHIO STATE**	2018 **CLEMSON**
2023 **MICHIGAN**	2017 **ALABAMA**
2022 **GEORGIA**	2016 **CLEMSON**
2021 **GEORGIA**	2015 **ALABAMA**
2020 **ALABAMA**	2014 **OHIO STATE**
2019 **LSU**	2013 **FLORIDA ST.**

Here's a handy guide to recent winners and champions of most of the major sports. They've all been celebrated in past editions of the YEAR IN SPORTS. But here they are all together again!

MLB

2024 Los Angeles **DODGERS** 4, New York **YANKEES** 1
2023 Texas **RANGERS** 4, Arizona **DIAMONDBACKS** 1
2022 Houston **ASTROS** 4, Philadelphia **PHILLIES** 2
2021 Atlanta **BRAVES** 4, Houston **ASTROS** 2
2020 Los Angeles **DODGERS** 4, Tampa Bay **RAYS** 2
2019 Washington **NATIONALS** 4, Houston **ASTROS** 3
2018 Boston **RED SOX** 4, Los Angeles **DODGERS** 1
2017 Houston **ASTROS** 4, Los Angeles **DODGERS** 3
2016 Chicago **CUBS** 4, Cleveland **INDIANS** 3
2015 Kansas City **ROYALS** 4, New York **METS** 1
2014 San Francisco **GIANTS** 4, Kansas City **ROYALS** 3

MLB MOST VALUABLE PLAYER

	AL	NL
2024	AARON **JUDGE**	SHOHEI **OHTANI**
2023	SHOHEI **OHTANI**	RONALD **ACUÑA JR.**
2022	AARON **JUDGE**	PAUL **GOLDSCHMIDT**
2021	SHOHEI **OHTANI**	BRYCE **HARPER**
2020	JOSÉ **ABREU**	FREDDIE **FREEMAN**
2019	MIKE **TROUT**	CODY **BELLINGER**
2018	MOOKIE **BETTS**	CHRISTIAN **YELICH**
2017	JOSÉ **ALTUVE**	GIANCARLO **STANTON**
2016	MIKE **TROUT**	KRIS **BRYANT**
2015	JOSH **DONALDSON**	BRYCE **HARPER**

COLLEGE BASKETBALL

YEAR	MEN'S	WOMEN'S
2025	Florida	Connecticut
2024	Connecticut	S. Carolina
2023	Connecticut	LSU
2022	Kansas	S. Carolina
2021	Baylor	Stanford
2020	Not played	Not played
2019	Virginia	Baylor
2018	Villanova	Notre Dame
2017	N. Carolina	S. Carolina
2016	Villanova	Connecticut
2015	Duke	Connecticut
2014	Connecticut	Connecticut

NHL

2025	**PANTHERS 4**, OILERS 2
2024	**PANTHERS 4**, CANUCKS 3
2023	**GOLDEN KNIGHTS 4**, PANTHERS 1
2022	**AVALANCHE 4**, LIGHTNING 2
2021	**LIGHTNING 4**, CANADIENS 1
2020	**LIGHTNING 4**, STARS 2
2019	**BLUES 4**, BRUINS 3
2018	**CAPITALS 4**, GOLDEN KNIGHTS 1
2017	**PENGUINS 4**, PREDATORS 2
2016	**PENGUINS 4**, SHARKS 2

PWHL

2025	**MINNESOTA 3**, Ottawa 1
2024	**MINNESOTA 3**, Boston 2

Breanna Stewart, a Liberty champ

NBA

2025	**Oklahoma City Thunder**
2024	**Boston Celtics**
2023	**Denver Nuggets**
2022	**Golden State Warriors**
2021	**Milwaukee Bucks**
2020	**Los Angeles Lakers**
2019	**Toronto Raptors**
2018	**Golden State Warriors**
2017	**Golden State Warriors**
2016	**Cleveland Cavaliers**
2015	**Golden State Warriors**

WNBA

2025	______________________
2024	**New York Liberty**
2023	**Las Vegas Aces**
2022	**Las Vegas Aces**
2021	**Chicago Sky**
2020	**Seattle Storm**
2019	**Washington Mystics**
2018	**Seattle Storm**
2017	**Minnesota Lynx**
2016	**Los Angeles Sparks**
2015	**Minnesota Lynx**

MLS

2024	**LA Galaxy**
2023	**Columbus Crew**
2022	**LAFC**
2021	**New York City FC**
2020	**Columbus Crew**
2019	**Seattle Sounders FC**
2018	**Atlanta United**
2017	**Toronto FC**

NWSL

2024	**Orlando Pride**
2023	**NY/NJ Gotham FC**
2022	**Portland Thorns**
2021	**Washington Spirit**
2020	**Canceled**
2019	**North Carolina Courage**
2018	**North Carolina Courage**
2017	**Portland Thorns FC**

FIFA WORLD PLAYER OF THE YEAR*

Year	Men	Women
2024	Vinícius **Júnior**	Aitana **Bonmatí**
2023	Lionel **Messi**	Aitana **Bonmatí**
2022	Lionel **Messi**	Alexia **Putellas**
2021	Robert **Lewandowski**	Alexia **Putellas**
2020	Robert **Lewandowski**	Lucy **Bronze**
2019	Lionel **Messi**	Megan **Rapinoe**#
2018	Luka **Modrić**	**Marta**
2017	Cristiano **Ronaldo**	Lieke **Martens**
2016	Cristiano **Ronaldo**	Carli **Lloyd**#
2015	Lionel **Messi**	Carli **Lloyd**#

* was known as the FIFA Ballon d'Or [Golden Ball] from 2010 to 2015. # from the United States

PGA PLAYER OF THE YEAR

Year	Player
2024	Scottie **Scheffler**
2023	Scottie **Scheffler**
2022	Scottie **Scheffler**
2021	Patrick **Cantlay**
2020	Dustin **Johnson**
2019	Rory **McIlroy**
2018	Brooks **Koepka**
2017	Justin **Thomas**
2016	Dustin **Johnson**
2015	Jordan **Spieth**
2014	Rory **McIlroy**

LPGA PLAYER OF THE YEAR

Year	Player
2024	Nelly **Korda**
2023	Lilia **Vu**
2022	Lydia **Ko**
2021	Jin Young **Ko**
2020	Sei Young **Kim**
2019	Jin Young **Ko**
2018	Ariya **Jutanugarn**
2017	Sung Hyun **Park** and So Yeon **Ryu**
2016	Ariya **Jutanugarn**
2015	Lydia **Ko**
2014	Stacy **Lewis**

ATP PLAYER OF THE YEAR

Year	Player
2024	Jannik SINNER
2023	Novak DJOKOVIC
2022	Carlos ALCARAZ
2021	Novak DJOKOVIC
2020	Novak DJOKOVIC
2019	Rafael NADAL
2018	Novak DJOKOVIC
2017	Rafael NADAL
2016	Andy MURRAY
2015	Novak DJOKOVIC
2014	Novak DJOKOVIC

WTA PLAYER OF THE YEAR

Year	Player
2024	Aryna SABALENKA
2023	Iga ŚWIĄTEK
2022	Iga ŚWIĄTEK
2021	Ashleigh BARTY
2020	Sofia KENIN
2019	Ashleigh BARTY
2018	Simona HALEP
2017	Garbiñe MUGURUZA
2016	Angelique KERBER
2015	Serena WILLIAMS
2014	Serena WILLIAMS

NASCAR

2024	JOEY **LOGANO**
2023	RYAN **BLANEY**
2022	JOEY **LOGANO**
2021	KYLE **LARSON**
2020	CHASE **ELLIOT**
2019	KYLE **BUSCH**
2018	JOEY **LOGANO**
2017	MARTIN **TRUEX JR.**
2016	JIMMIE **JOHNSON**
2015	KYLE **BUSCH**
2014	KEVIN **HARVICK**
2013	JIMMIE **JOHNSON**

INDYCAR

2024	ÁLEX **PALOU**
2023	ÁLEX **PALOU**
2022	WILL **POWER**
2021	ÁLEX **PALOU**
2020	SCOTT **DIXON**
2019	JOSEF **NEWGARDEN**
2018	SCOTT **DIXON**
2017	JOSEF **NEWGARDEN**
2016	SIMON **PAGENAUD**
2015	SCOTT **DIXON**
2014	WILL **POWER**
2013	SCOTT **DIXON**

FORMULA 1

2024	MAX **VERSTAPPEN**
2023	MAX **VERSTAPPEN**
2022	MAX **VERSTAPPEN**
2021	MAX **VERSTAPPEN**
2020	LEWIS **HAMILTON**
2019	LEWIS **HAMILTON**
2018	LEWIS **HAMILTON**

DAYTONA 500 CHAMPIONS

2025	**Will BYRON**
2024	**Will BYRON**
2023	**Ricky STENHOUSE JR.**
2022	**Austin CINDRIC**
2021	**Michael MCDOWELL**
2020	**Denny HAMLIN**
2019	**Denny HAMLIN**
2018	**Austin DILLON**
2017	**Kurt BUSCH**
2016	**Denny HAMLIN**

INDY 500 CHAMPIONS

2025	**Álex PALOU**
2024	**Josef NEWGARDEN**
2023	**Josef NEWGARDEN**
2022	**Marcus ERICSSON**
2021	**Hélio CASTRONEVES**
2020	**Takuma SATO**
2019	**Simon PAGENAUD**
2018	**Will POWER**
2017	**Takuma SATO**
2016	**Alexander ROSSI**

Logano was NASCAR's No. 1.

Produced by Shoreline Publishing Group LLC
Santa Barbara, California
www.shorelinepublishing.com
President/Editorial Director: James Buckley, Jr.
Designed by Tom Carling, www.carlingdesign.com

The text for *Scholastic Year in Sports 2026* was written by
James Buckley, Jr.
Other writers: **Jim Gigliotti** (Golf and Tennis); **Beth Adelman** and **Craig Zeichner** (NHL); **Jacob Norling** (College Basketball), and **John Clendening** (College Football).
Fact-checking: **Matt Marini** and **Ken Samelson**. Proofreading: **Elizabeth Sullivan**. Thanks to all!
Thanks to team captain **Tiffany Colón**, the photo squad of **Emily Teresa** and **Marybeth Kavanagh**, and the superstars at Scholastic for all their championship work!
Photo research was done by the author.

Photography Credits

Photos ©: cover top left: Bruce Bennett/Getty Images; cover top right: Megan Briggs/Getty Images; cover center far left: Liverpool FC/Liverpool FC via Getty Images; cover center left: Sam Hodde/Getty Images; cover center: Reginald Mathalone/NurPhoto via Getty Images; cover center right: Joe Buglewicz/Getty Images; cover center far right: Dan Hamilton-Imagn Images; cover bottom left: Melissa Tamez/Icon Sportswire via Getty Images; cover bottom center: Cooper Neill/Getty Images; cover bottom right: M. Anthony Nesmith/Icon Sportswire via Getty Images; cover background: Shutterstock.com; back cover top left: Al Sermeno/ISI Photos/Getty Images; back cover top right: Jurij Kodrun/International Skating Union via Getty Images; back cover bottom: Michael Hickey/Getty Images; 4: Grace Hollars/IndyStar/USA TODAY NETWORK via Imagn Images; 5: Mark J. Rebilas-Imagn Images; 6: Mark J. Rebilas-Imagn Images; 7 top: Soobum Im/Getty Images; 7 bottom: The Cincinnati Enquirer-Imagn Images; 8 top: Giuseppe Maffia/DeFodi Images via Getty Images; 8 bottom: Ed Mulholland-Imagn Images; 9 top: AP Photo/Matt Rourke; 9 bottom: Jamie Schwaberow/NCAA Photos/Getty Images; 10 top: James Gilbert/Getty Images; 10 bottom: AP Photo/Duane Burleson; 11 top: AP Photo/Matt Slocum; 11 bottom: Kim Klement Neitzel-Imagn Images; 12 top: Steph Chambers/Getty Images; 12 bottom: AP Photo/Julia Demaree Nikhinson; 13 top: Beata Zawrzel/Anadolu via Getty Images; 13 bottom: Yeshiva University Athletics; 14: Xinhua News Agency/Getty Images; 15: Mauro Ujetto/NurPhoto/Getty Images; 16 top: Steph Chambers/Getty Images; 16 bottom: Alex Davidson/Getty Images; 17 top: Alex Slitz/Getty Images; 17 bottom: Steph Chambers/Getty Images; 18–19: Kiyoshi Mio-Imagn Images; 20: Junfu Han/USA TODAY NETWORK via Imagn Images; 21: Peter Aiken-Imagn Images; 22: Rich von Biberstein/Icon Sportswire/AP Images; 23 top: AP Photo/Rich Schultz; 23 bottom: Charles LeClaire-Imagn Images; 24 top: Gregory Fisher/Icon Sportswire/AP Images; 24 bottom: Mary DeCicco/MLB Photos/Getty Images; 25 top: Katelyn Mulcahy/Getty Images; 25 bottom: Brian Rothmuller/Icon Sportswire/Getty Images; 26: AP Photo/Paul Sancya; 27 top: J. Conrad Williams Jr./Newsday RM/Getty Images; 27 bottom: Robert Gauthier/Los Angeles Times/Getty Images; 28: AP Photo/Mark J. Terrill; 29: Dustin Satloff/MLB Photos/Getty Images; 30: Brad Penner-Imagn Images; 31: Michael Reaves/Getty Images; 32: Brett Rojo-Imagn Images; 33 top: Steven Branscombe-Imagn Images; 33 bottom: Steven Branscombe-Imagn Images; 34–35: AP Photo/David J. Phillip; 36: Perry Knotts/Getty Images; 37: Todd Rosenberg/AP Photo; 38: Tim Heitman-Imagn Images; 39: Aaron M. Sprecher/AP Photo; 40: Logan Bowles/AP Photo; 41: Kara Durrette/AP Photo; 42: AP Photo/Chris Szagola; 43: Lauren Leigh Bacho/Getty Images; 44: Katelyn Mulcahy/Getty Images; 45: Jayne Kamin-Oncea-Imagn Images; 46: Paul Spinelli/AP Photo; 47: Thomas Shea-Imagn Images; 48: Paul Spinelli/AP Photo; 49: Jorge Lemus/NurPhoto via Getty Images; 50: Aaron M. Sprecher/AP Photo; 51 top: Emilee Chinn/Getty Images; 51 bottom: Geoff Burke-Imagn Images; 52: AP Photo/Godofredo A. Vásquez; 53 top: Mark J. Rebilas-Imagn Images; 53 bottom: AP Photo/Matt Slocum; 54: Eric Hartline-Imagn Images; 55: Dylan Buell/Getty Images; 56 top: Ian Maule/Getty Images; 56 bottom: Samuel Teets- USA Football; 57 top: AP Photo/Genevieve Ross; 57 bottom: Damian Strohmeyer/AP Photo; 58–59: Adam Cairns/Columbus Dispatch/USA TODAY NETWORK via Imagn Images; 60: Darryl Oumi/Getty Images; 61: Robert Hanashiro-Imagn Images; 62: Christopher Hanewinckel-Imagn Images; 63: John David Mercer-Imagn Images; 64: Carly Mackler/Getty Images; 65 top: Steve Limentani/ISI Photos/Getty Images; 65 bottom: Brent Gudenschwager/Cal Sport Media/AP Images; 66: Jeremy Hogan / SOPA Images/Sipa USA/AP Images; 67 top: Junfu Han / USA TODAY NETWORK via Imagn Images; 67 bottom: Tommy Gilligan-Imagn Images; 68: Perry McIntyre/ISI Photos/Getty Images; 69: Lauren Witte/Clarion Ledger/USA TODAY NETWORK via Imagn Images; 70: Tim Warner/Getty Images; 71: Samantha Madar/USA TODAY NETWORK via Imagn Images; 72: Mark J. Rebilas-Imagn Images; 73: Kyle Robertson/Columbus Dispatch/USA TODAY NETWORK via Imagn Images; 74: Alex Slitz/Getty Images; 75 top: AP Photo/Jacob Kupferman; 75 bottom: John Adams/Icon Sportswire/Getty Images; 76: Scott Winters/Icon Sportswire/Getty Images; 77: AP Photo/Julio Cortez; 78: AP Photo/Pamela Smith; 79: Alonzo Adams-Imagn Images; 80: Wendell Cruz-Imagn Images; 81: M. Anthony Nesmith/Icon Sportswire/AP Images; 82: Melissa Tamez/Icon Sportswire/AP Images; 83 top: AP Photo/Ross D. Franklin; 83 bottom: Michael Chow/The Republic/USA TODAY NETWORK via Imagn Images; 84: AP Photo/Michael Conroy; 85: Melissa Tamez/Icon Sportswire/AP Images; 86: AP Photo/Corey Sipkin; 87: AP Photo/Jessica Hill; 88: AP Photo/Abbie Parr; 89: AP Photo/Pamela Smith; 90: Kamil Krzaczynski-Imagn Images; 91: Mark J. Rebilas-Imagn Images; 92: Jerome Miron-Imagn Images; 93: Jason Parkhurst-Imagn Images; 94: Brad Penner-Imagn Images; 95 top: AP Photo/Ian Maule; 95 bottom: Ron Chenoy-Imagn Images; 96: Cary Edmondson-Imagn Images; 97: Alonzo Adams-Imagn Images; 98: AP Photo/Julio Cortez; 99 top: AP Photo/Nate Billings; 99 bottom: AP Photo/Kyle Phillips; 100: Jeff Hanisch-Imagn Images; 101: AP Photo/Rick Scuteri; 102: Nathan Ray Seebeck-Imagn Images; 103: Robert Deutsch-Imagn Images; 104: Rich Barnes-Imagn Images; 105: Robert Hanashiro-Imagn Images; 106: Ken Ruinard-Imagn Images; 107: Caitie McMekin/News Sentinel/USA TODAY NETWORK via Imagn Images; 108: Bryan Lynn/Icon Sportswire/AP Images; 109 top: AP Photo/Michael Conroy; 109 bottom: AP Photo/Steve Conner; 110 top: Eric Canha-Imagn Images; 110 bottom: AP Photo/Charles Krupa; 111: AP Photo/Ryan Sun; 112: AP Photo/Brynn Anderson; 113: Alex Slitz/Getty Images; 114 left: David Butler II-Imagn Images; 114 right: Gregory Fisher-Imagn Images; 115: Daniel Kucin Jr.-Imagn Images; 116 top: Kirby Lee-Imagn Images; 116 bottom: Maddie Meyer/Getty Images; 117 left: Ben Solomon/NCAA Photos via Getty Images; 117 right: Jeff Blake-Imagn Images; 118–119: Sam Navarro-Imagn Images; 119 inset: Steven Garcia/Cal Sport Media/AP Images; 120 top: AP Photo/Mark Stockwell; 120 bottom: Geoff Burke-Imagn Images; 121: Maddie Meyer/Getty Images; 122: Fred Greenslade/The Canadian Press/AP Photo; 123 top: Sam Hodde/Getty Images; 123 bottom: James Guillory-Imagn Images; 124: Codie McLachlan/Getty Images; 125 top: Jeff Vinnick/Getty Images; 125 bottom: Peter Joneleit/Icon Sportswire/Getty Images; 126: Mark LoMoglio/NHLI/Getty Images; 127: Nathan Denette/The Canadian Press/AP Images; 128 top: Rich Graessle/Getty Images; 128 bottom: AP Photo/Petr David Josek; 129: Troy Parla/Getty Images; 130: Graham Hughes/The Canadian Press/AP Photo; 131: Steven Garcia/Cal Sport Media/AP Images; 132-133: Angel Martinez - UEFA/UEFA/Getty Images; 134: Stephen M. Dowell/Orlando Sentinel/Tribune News Service/Getty Images; 135: Rich Graessle/Icon Sportswire/Getty Images; 136 top: Meg Oliphant/Getty Images; 136 bottom: Maria Lysaker-Imagn Images; 137 top: Katharine Lotze/Getty Images; 137 bottom: Steven Bisig-Imagn Images; 138: Geoff Burke-Imagn Images; 139 top: Denny Medley-Imagn Images; 139 bottom: Jay Biggerstaff-Imagn Images; 140: Simon Bruty/Anychance/Getty Images; 141: Kirby Lee-Imagn Images; 142: Mike Watters-Imagn Images; 143: Shaun Clark/ISI Photos/Getty Images; 144: Ulrik Pedersen/NurPhoto via Getty Images; 145 top: Jose Breton/Pics Action/NurPhoto via Getty Images; 145 bottom: Justin Setterfield/Getty Images; 146: Elianton/Mondadori Portfolio via Getty Images; 147: Jürgen Fromme - firo sportphoto/Getty Images; 148: Joan Valls/Urbanandsport/NurPhoto via Getty Images; 148–149: Catherine Ivill - AMA/Getty Images; 149: Joan Valls/Urbanandsport/NurPhoto via Getty Images; 150: Chris Brunskill/Fantasista/Getty Images; 151: Francesco Pecoraro/Getty Images; 152 top: Harriet Lander - Chelsea FC/Chelsea FC via Getty Images; 152 bottom: Charlie Crowhurst - The FA/The FA via Getty Images; 153 top: Marco Steinbrenner/DeFodi Images/DeFodi/Getty Images; 153 bottom: Harry Langer/picture alliance/Getty Images; 154: Sean Gardner/Getty Images; 155: Chris Leduc/Icon Sportswire/Getty Images; 156: AP Photo/Butch Dill; 157 top: Michael Bush/Icon Sportswire/AP Images; 157 bottom: Jared C. Tilton/Getty Images; 158 left: Sean Gardner/Getty Images; 158 right: Meg Oliphant/Getty Images; 159 top: Sean Gardner/Getty Images; 159 bottom: Kevin Abele/Icon Sportswire/AP Images; 160: Andy Hone/LAT Images; 161 top: Clive Mason/Getty Images; 161 center: Kym Illman/Getty Images; 162 inset: Michael Allio/Icon Sportswire/Getty Images; 162 bottom: Mike Wulf/Cal Sport Media/AP Images; 163 top: Dan Hamilton-Imagn Images; 163 bottom: Butch Dill-Imagn Images; 164: Justin Cooper/Cal Sport Media/AP Images; 165 top: David J. Griffin/Icon Sportswire/AP Images; 165 bottom: Brian Spurlock/Icon Sportswire/AP Images; 166 top: Aaron Doster-Imagn Images; 166 bottom: Vincent Ethier/Icon Sportswire/AP Images; 167 top: GREG LOVETT/PALM BEACH POST/USA TODAY NETWORK via Imagn Images; 167 bottom: AP Photo/Phelan M. Ebenhack; 168: Kyle Terada-Imagn Images; 169: Alex Slitz/Getty Images; 170: Tnani Badreddine/DeFodi Images/Getty Images; 171: Nicolò Campo/LightRocket/Getty Images; 172: AP Photo/Ng Han Guan; 173: Clive Brunskill/Getty Images; 174 top: Jean Catuffe/Getty Images; 174 bottom: Ethan Miller/Getty Images; 175 top: Li Jing/Xinhua via Getty Images; 175 bottom: Cynthia Lum/Icon Sportswire/Corbis/Getty Images; 176: Maddie Meyer/Getty Images; 177: Mauro Ujetto/NurPhoto via Getty Images; 178 top: Ezra Shaw/Getty Images; 178 bottom: Ezra Shaw/Getty Images; 179 top: Ezra Shaw/Getty Images; 179 bottom: Kyodo/AP Images; 180: Kirby Lee/AP Images; 181: Joe Robbins/NCAA Photos/NCAA Photos/Getty Images; 182: Gregory Fisher-Imagn Images; 183 top: Terence Lewis/Icon Sportswire via Getty Images; 183 bottom: Darrin Fry/UFA; 184 top: Rouelle Umali/Xinhua/Getty Images; 184 bottom: Major League Cricket; 185 top: Mouneb Taim/INA Photo Agency/Sipa USA/AP Images; 185 center: Borja B. Hojas/Getty Images; 185 bottom: Guven Yilmaz/Anadolu Agency via Getty Images; 186: Rich von Biberstein/Icon Sportswire/AP Images; 188: AP Photo/Pamela Smith; 191: Kevin Abele/Icon Sportswire/AP Images.